At Least I Tried

Kevin Kindelin

Contents

Chapter 1: Hospitalization and Rehabilitation

A mirror reflecting my acne-ridden face is the first thing I can remember when I realized I was paralyzed. There was a mirror positioned above me so I could see my face and other angles because I couldn't move my head. I saw these tongs drilled into my temples that secured the weights that kept me in traction. I could feel my whole body from head to toe, but I couldn't move a thing. I knew I was paralyzed from a spinal cord injury, but I didn't know how I knew. I just knew. So here I am, 19 years old; I know I'm paralyzed, but the thing that bothers me the most at the time was a new case of severe acne. I was shocked! I was pretty much past the pimple stage. I vaguely remember that I was told an injury to the spinal cord will create an influx of testosterone that somehow or another is the result of something or another that is supposed to come to the defense of something else. I thought I had grown up and matured into a tall, strapping young man. Seeing a face full of acne traumatized me for some reason.

The focus on my acne dissipated somewhat when the full realization of the consequences of my actions hit me. Apparently, so the story goes, I had done a handstand on a second story balcony railing as I was leaving a college party. I guess it was a party of fellow rugby players, friends, and girlfriends who made up the regular crew of crazies. From what I was told, I was almost three times the legal limit for blood alcohol. The legal limit at that time was 0.10 in contrast to today's 0.08 limit. The one eyewitness to the fall said I was doing a handstand but lost it and plummeted to the sidewalk below. I sustained a cervical six spinal cord injury...meaning I broke my neck. The impact shattered the fifth, sixth, and seventh vertebrae but it seemed like the damage to the spinal cord itself wasn't as bad as it could have been. Nevertheless, I was paralyzed from my chest down, along with my hands and parts of my arms. I still had full function of my shoulder muscles (deltoids) and biceps. The vertebrae in my neck had to be fused together with a piece of bone that was taken from my hip to support the fractured shards of bone left floating around my spinal cord awaiting surgery. It was called an incomplete injury, as the spinal cord wasn't completely severed or crushed. This gave me the hope that someday I would be able to rehabilitate and recover, that somehow the spinal cord tissue would regenerate and heal. The doctors didn't completely rule it out, but they said it was extremely doubtful. That hope, albeit false hope in the end, helped me to hang on, then and for years afterward.

At the beginning of my sophomore year at Illinois State University, I decided to go out for the rugby club. At 19, I had developed into a tall, well-muscled, very fast, gifted athlete. During my freshman year, my friends and I formed an intramural football team. It was just a bunch of guys from my dorm who competed against other students who put together teams from the dorms, fraternities, and even off campus. This is how I met Ken

Henry, my future housemate, rugby player, and fastest person that I had ever known personally. He was the only guy I knew who was faster than me. His short, piston-like legs always churned him across the finish line a step ahead of me in a full-out sprint. Ken encouraged me to come out for the rugby club, while at the same time, a couple of guys from the football team tried to get me to try out for the varsity football team. Illinois State University was a division one school, but it wasn't a football powerhouse. I thought I would be able to make the team, but I probably wouldn't start since I didn't play in high school. That's a topic for a little later. So I joined the rugby club and began learning an entirely new sport. It's the daddy of football, but very different. The point of my braggadocio is that I went from this physically-gifted person whose body would do almost anything that was asked of it to a person who couldn't move at all. In an instant, it was gone, never to be regained, although I refused to believe that at the time. It was an instant of which I had, and still have, no memory.

The blow to my head wiped out my

memory from the week before my accident through the week after. From what I was told, I was conscious and conversing with people a few days after, but I wasn't lucid and I have no memory of those conversations. I think that's where I learned I had broken my neck and was paralyzed. The doctors must have told me but I have no memory of any such conversation. Initially, they had me in a Stryker bed, which rotated backward to frontward that allowed for some pressure relief but seemed like a major undertaking and was somewhat of a freak show from my perspective. There was even one mishap when I was rotating forward and had started to slip at the apex of the rotation. Apparently, the nurse who strapped on the front piece I would lie on while I was lying on my stomach did not strap it in tightly enough. She was horrified and quite beside herself, but the doctor assured all of us that no further damage had been done. I was already pretty messed up!

The surgery that would fuse my vertebrae had to be delayed due to a kidney infection. My whole mindset was on getting the surgery done so I could start rehabilitating and eventually walk again. There was no other choice. I was a rough, tough, fighting Irishman who was not going to take this lying down! I was determined that I was going to win this fight. What an irony! What a joke! Here I was lying flat on my back, helpless as a baby, struggling to maintain a semblance of manhood. I don't recall praying, even though I did have the proverbial mustard seed of faith planted in me during my Catholic upbringing. I was going to do it all. I was going to show everyone. I was quickly humbled and fell into a deep depression when I couldn't deny the reality and permanence of my situation. Still, I held onto a glimmer of hope that someday I would get up and walk. But at that moment, I knew I was screwed!

After two weeks, my kidney infection finally relented and I was able to have the fusion surgery. Soon after, the goal was to get me into a wheelchair and as functional as possible. That wouldn't happen at this hospital, but the process of re-learning how to use my body in every conceivable way one can imagine began its lifelong, never ending journey there. When a person injures one's spinal cord, the central nervous system sustains damage akin to crossing wires in an electrical system. Doing so can result in unexpected surprises. One of the first steps of my rehabilitation was to get my body acclimated to being somewhat vertical rather than horizontal as I had been for the past several weeks. To do this, I was strapped to a table that tilted from horizontal to vertical in varying and increasing degrees. Even the circulation and the ability to pump blood, and thereby oxygen, to my brain was compromised. If I were tilted vertically too quickly or too much, I could quite easily pass out. I don't remember too much of this process except for one time when I was tilted to an increased vertical position and I crapped all over the place! The dam burst open of my long dormant bowels. The spinal cord injury itself temporarily paralyzed the normal peristalsis process, but the narcotics and other drugs coursing through my system really shut things down. The only thing that was done for that process for the time being was this cutout in the bed where my butt was that had a collection bucket or pan of sorts attached underneath to catch the poop. Ironically, the ridge in the cutout actually caused my first pressure sore that took many months to heal.

Suffice it to say, I was horrified and embarrassed by my sudden incontinence. I would have to relearn how to use my bowels as well as my bladder. I had been catheterized since being hospitalized and the goal was to wean me off the indwelling catheter, but that would be a long and difficult process. I would have to relearn how to use the muscles that weren't paralyzed, and also use them to substitute for some muscles that were. The intense physical therapy it would take to achieve that would have to wait until I was discharged from the trauma center and admitted to a rehabilitation facility.

A big part of this journey was, has been, and still is, my family and friends. They traveled to Peoria from the Chicago suburbs and back many times over the course of the two months that I was a patient at Saint Francis Hospital. It was the closest trauma center to ISU. The hospital had dorm type facilities where family members and friends could stay overnight if necessary. It was a very old building and more than one of my family members commented that they felt like the place was haunted. Regardless, they would stay overnight many times over those two months. This occurred several years before the iconic movie, but they weren't afraid of no ghosts!

The accident happened in the wee hours of November 10, 1979, so Thanksgiving, and Christmas were not so festive or merry that year. Even with the support and love from my family, I was deeply depressed and lost my appetite, as I recall. Someone in my family would go out to the best places around, even picking up delicious, rare steaks, one of my favorite meals. I would try to eat but I just couldn't. My weight dropped to 120 pounds. At 6 foot 3, I looked like a skeleton, much to my mother's horror. She commented for many years afterward, "I could count your ribs!"

By the end of December, the rehabilitation was going nowhere as this was a trauma center and not equipped for the extensive rehabilitative processes I needed. Of course, they wouldn't discharge me until I was stable enough. I was waiting to be transferred to the Rehabilitation Institute of Chicago (RIC), which I was told was the best rehabilitation hospital in the country. All I could think of was getting there and learning how to walk again. Simple as that. All I had to do was work hard enough and everything would come back. I expected hard work, but I didn't expect the ensuing frustration. The first frustration in this next step was waiting for a bed to open up at the RIC, so my parents had me transferred to the Alexian Brothers Medical Center in Elk Grove, which was just a few miles from their home. I was admitted to the rehabilitation wing of the hospital but I wasn't there very long, and didn't get much accomplished before I was transferred to the RIC.

I remember very well that I was not in a good mood as I began the next phase of my new life, a life that for the next four months consisted of re-learning how to use some parts of my body and learning how to use other parts to substitute for those parts that would not work. This hospital was very different in that patients didn't stay in their rooms and languish. We would have our therapies in large common areas where we could all see our successes and failures as we tried to progress through various stages of rehabilitation. There were no TVs in our rooms back then. There was one TV in a common area for all to watch. As this was 1980, the winter Olympics were on, but I was overruled in favor of "BJ and the Bear!" If you remember, that was a TV show about a truck driver who traveled around the country with a chimpanzee as a companion. I missed the "Miracle on Ice" because of a chump chimp!

For our meals, we had the choice of eating in the common area adjacent to the TV room, or we could go to the hospital cafeteria on the second floor where hospital staff, guests, and everybody else would eat. When I arrived there in January, I was just learning how to get my hands to my mouth. I had no desire to spill food all over myself in such a public setting. The goal was to get patients to interact with each other and other people as we transitioned back into our lives outside of hospitals. I know my bad mood was due to what I thought was a lack of progress. My mood would have to change if I were to get along with those around me.

As this was practically going to be my home for the next four months, I had to acclimate to my surroundings and "go with the program." I wanted to do whatever it took to get better. Patients were assigned a case nurse who would oversee each patient's progress, as well as overall well being. My nurse was Peggy Green. She was only a few years older than me but seemed a lot wiser. She was blonde and pretty and even my mom said she had a cute butt. More importantly, she was dedicated to helping patients regain their lives. She was kind and understanding, but was also very intense. She was demanding, but she only demanded what she thought her patients could handle. Peggy motivated and challenged me in many ways. She recognized my competitive nature and would often manipulate that to get the best out of me. I would get so frustrated with myself, especially in the first weeks when I was confined to a gurney type cart that I had to lie on and try to push around. It had wheelchair type wheels attached to each side that allowed me to propel myself around a bit. The pressure store on my tail bone was preventing me from transitioning to a wheelchair. As I was falling into another bout of depression, the staff made the decision to get me upright and into a wheelchair. I was just re-learning how to use my shoulders and the muscles that were still functioning in my arms, primarily the biceps and one of the forearm muscles in each arm. My hands were paralyzed and basically relegated to paws.

I met some interesting people from various and diverse cultures and backgrounds. My roommate was a good ole southern boy from Kentucky, if I remember correctly. He was racing his car when it flipped and caused extensive head injuries. His name was Steve Smith but he went by "Snuffy," as in the comic strip character. He couldn't speak anymore and his paralyzed body was twisted and contorted. His intellect was still there but he could only communicate with a spelling board that was quite primitive by today's standards. Gilberto "Gil" Aldaco was a young man from the gang-controlled neighborhoods of Chicago who had been shot in the back in a drive-by shooting by a rival gang. Gil was only paralyzed from the waist down, so he was in the best condition of the three of us. We made up an unlikely trio who would hang out and talk in Snuffy's and my room when it was time for us to get out of our chairs, mainly for pressure relief. Neither one of us could lift ourselves from our chairs to adequately employ enough pressure relief to avoid the dreaded sores. Snuffy could only make unintelligible noises when he tried to speak, but his vociferous acknowledgment of the subject matter, be it negative or positive, was quite clear. He was able to spell out what he wanted to say, but since I couldn't see his board from my bed, Gil would roll over between the two beds and vocalize what Snuffy was trying to spell. On more than one occasion, Snuffy said he wanted to kill himself.

Most of the patients at the RIC were young men. There were a few female patients, but the statistics showed there were more young men who got themselves into situations that required such extensive rehabilitation. Certainly, there were some patients with organic conditions such as strokes, heart attacks, neurological disorders, etc., but most were young males who were there due to some type of accident.

The spinal cord is the messaging conduit of the central nervous system that carries the signals from the brain to the various reaches and extremities of the body to carry out the complex set of interrelated functions that make the human body do what it does. Injuring the spinal cord creates a host of problems, seen and unseen, that rebel against one's very own body. My constant companion, but definitely not my friend, has been pain. It's a very strange type of pain coursing through my body at all times that I cannot describe in "able-bodied terms." I can't compare it to anything I felt before I was injured. It's kind of like an electrical charge of sorts. I have learned to compartmentalize it in order to tolerate it aside from any newborn pain. None of the narcotics that were prescribed to me did any good, so I gave them up a long time ago. Muscle spasms joined the entourage of rebellion and could be quite painful in and of themselves. The spasms could run from mild to severe and would affect the paralyzed muscles, which of course were most of the muscles in my body. The worst ones were the ones that ran up and down my abdomen and lower back. It felt like I was being punched from the inside out. I had never before felt anything like it.

I mentioned earlier that I would need to learn how to retrain my bladder. Up until then, I had an indwelling catheter known as a Foley catheter doing all the work of voiding the urine. The goal was to get the bladder to work on its own by removing the Foley catheter and intermittently catheterizing every four hours until the bladder could function on its own. It wasn't a pleasant process as I had full sensation there. The doctors wanted me to push the liquids to stimulate my kidneys to fill up my bladder every few hours. I wasn't in the mood to follow their directions but I remember telling them that if they let me drink beer in their hospital, then I would push my liquids. Surprisingly, they allowed it, but I had to drink the beer out of a paper cup with a straw so the other patients wouldn't know that it was beer. I was still learning how to use my arms and hands again, so picking up a can or bottle of beer was not a physical possibility yet anyway!

I called them my hands, but at this point they functioned more like paws. It was difficult to get my hands around objects, especially cups or glasses. Because my fingers and two of the three major muscles in each forearm didn't work, I had to learn new techniques utilizing different muscles and or adaptives to accomplish even the simplest of tasks. It's called substitution. Every movement began with a calculation. I would need to learn how to substitute my deltoids for my triceps (muscle group in the back of the arm). We use our triceps to extend our arms which is important for pressure relief from sitting in the wheelchair. This would prove to be problematic over the years as substituting deltoids for the triceps was never enough. One of the most important techniques I learned is called tenodesis. By lifting my hand with the one muscle in my forearm still functioning, it naturally draws the index finger and thumb together creating a "false grip." It would take a lot of exercise and practice to make this work. My right hand was virtually useless... good thing I'm a lefty! I was having a difficult time learning this technique. The first time I was able to pick anything up, I was at a little celebration that a few patients, friends, and family members were having for a soon-to-be discharged patient who had also become a friend. It was technically against the rules, but they looked the other way when we snuck in some booze.

At one point during the celebration, I reached down and picked up an empty Styrofoam cup. It was the first time I would pick up something without an adaptive ratchet splint on my arm and hand. Everybody at the table cheered. I, on the other hand, clearly remember being so disgusted with myself that I slammed the cup down in a huff. How could they be cheering for such a mere accomplishment as picking up an empty Styrofoam cup? There was so much I had to do. There was so much more I **needed** to do! I know my anger was an immature emotion. They were only trying to encourage me, but I was driven by self-directed anger. I was never happy with anything I accomplished then, and I guess the same is true now.

Rehabilitation would continue to be an arduous, frustrating, yet extremely educational process. I did learn quite a bit, but any and all medical information I present is strictly from a layman's point of view. I would have to learn so much about how my body worked so I could function with a body that didn't really work all that well anymore. I would learn little techniques and "'workarounds" in order to be able to accomplish some of life's little tasks. I tried to learn as much as I could so I would be able to function in the real world. It was frustrating and very depressing that I would now be dependent on another person or persons to be able to even get out of bed and go to the bathroom. Even so, I was going to do as much as I could to take care of myself. The most horrendous and humiliating aspect of all this was going to the bathroom. That's right, taking a crap! Things didn't work the same anymore. Things went when they wanted to go, not when I told them to, so things had to be retrained. It would start in the morning with a bisacodyl suppository. The nurse or aide that was assigned to me that morning would insert a suppository where the sun never shone before! I previously mentioned that I still had sensation in my body. I learned that the motor and sensory nerves are actually independent of each other and paralysis of one does not necessarily mean a lack of sensation in the other. Every case is different. In my case, I could feel all that and I didn't like it! The ingredients of the suppository were supposed to irritate the rectal lining which was supposed to induce peristalsis. Something I never thought of was how the poop that we carry around in our bodies is actually poison and very bad for us. Especially with a spinal cord injured body, a backed up or impacted bowel can lead to serious consequences. To this day, I do a variation of this process and it is still the worst part of my morning. I use a more efficient product than the bisacodyl suppository, though. I use what is called a mini enema which is basically just a small amount of some chemical that gets squirted up in there from a small plastic vial and does a better and faster job than the suppository. Regardless, over the years, my body has reacted to this process in more horrific ways than I could ever have imagined. Cold sweat. My body breaks out all over in a cold sweat as it does its business. I shake and shiver, even in warm weather. I am so thankful for hot showers! This didn't occur in the early years, but for the past 20 years or so it has become increasingly worse.

I was never really the shy type or embarrassed about being naked, but the amount that all of me was exposed so often was something that took getting used to. I was still able to get erections and as a 19 year old male, I got my share of them. At the beginning of each catheterization was a time when this would always occur. The nurse would either say nothing, or something like, "Don't worry. I'm used to it. It happens all the time." Well, I wasn't used to it! Then the catheter would slide through the urethra and hit the sphincter, where it would stop immediately. This was always very painful, even more so than the initial entry. It would usually take the nurse a few times to slightly withdraw the catheter and push it back again, banging on the sphincter like knocking on the front door. It would always open, but it was always very unpleasant! This was something I had to get used to and lose my inhibitions fast. Gil had to endure the same retraining as I did, and instead of admitting to our discomfort and embarrassment, we started calling this event our "date with Cathy." Going through my daily routine, I would have to be naked and exposed while I did my toileting function, bathed, and got dressed. I know now how much we take these things for granted and probably don't understand the value of privacy, but I've learned.

Chapter 2: Making Progress

After a couple of months of rehabilitation, I was allowed to go home on weekends. Someone had to be able to care for me, so members of my family had to be taught. I was mortified by the thought of my mother or sisters being involved in my personal care. That was one inhibition I couldn't get past. Nurses and aides seeing me in all my glory was one thing, my mom and sisters were another. My dad and my brother Kelly would assume these duties when I would come home, but I would only allow my mom and my sisters, Diana and Laura, to help with other non-personal things. Everybody wanted to help and I needed to be helped but I didn't want to be helped.

My family and close friends would often make the trip to downtown Chicago to visit me at the RIC. In so doing, we became friends with other patients and some of the staff, especially my nurse Peggy. Even after I was discharged, my brother, some of my friends, and I would sometimes go over to her apartment in Chicago for parties or go on an excursion to the zoo or some other place of interest. I don't believe in coincidence anymore, so I'll just say that Peggy had befriended and become roommates with Leslie Godula, who just happened to be a young spinal cord injured quadriplegic woman who was injured about 10 years earlier at the age of 15 in a diving accident. When Leslie was injured, they didn't know too much about rehabilitation, so she wasn't able to get the most out of whatever function was left in her body. Although our injuries were similar, our rehabilitation couldn't have been more different. Actually, Leslie's rehabilitation was nonexistent. Upon discharge from the hospital, she was placed in a bed with both her arms bent at the elbows so she could utilize her still functioning shoulder muscles to be able to reach her face. Still, her attitude was far better than mine ever was or would become, and her spirit was unquenchable. I learned a lot from this woman. She seemed to be at peace with herself, a peace I have never felt. I remember asking her how she did it. She said there's no choice. She just did.

My rehabilitation continued through the winter and spring months in early 1980. To be accurate, my rehabilitation has never stopped as I learn new things and new ways of accomplishing tasks along the way, but the "blueprint" of how I would basically function for the rest of my life was established then. With implements, adaptives, and devices of various sorts, I would learn new techniques to accomplish such basic life skills as eating, shaving, brushing my teeth, and signing my name to name a few. I never could coordinate my hand and arm well enough to write anything legibly, just a chicken scratch of a signature. Still, I knew I had to get myself in good enough and functional enough condition to be able to return to school. I knew I had to earn my degree if I were to have any semblance of a normal life. Even though I was still within my own window of hope to someday walk again, I knew I had to adapt to my current situation if I didn't want to live the rest of my life in a hospital bed.

The doctors and my parents consented to

a weekend trip to ISU to visit my friends and see a rugby match. Kelly went with me, and maybe another guy also, I don't remember exactly. But I do remember I had a great time, too great as it turned out. After the match, both rugby clubs, friends, and spectators gathered around a keg and sang traditional rugby songs and pretty much got hammered! I still wasn't strong enough to pick up a full beer cup, so a host of my buddies encircled me and poured beer down my gaping throat. I was singing and laughing and getting very drunk! I didn't realize the danger I was putting myself in. After the party, we went to the house I was living in just a few months prior to this triumphant return, or semi-return. Everything was cool with my ex-roommates, but a new guy occupied my former bedroom, so we all slept on the couches and floor. In the morning, I couldn't urinate, and I was sweating and had a tremendous headache that signaled the onset of hyper-reflexia. Kelly was trained to recognize the signs so he catheterized me with the emergency catheters Peggy made us bring. I remember protesting to the necessity, but Peggy got her way. Thank God. It saved my life. By the time I would have been able to get to the hospital, my bladder would have burst and poisoned my system on the way to a very unpleasant demise. The urine he catheterized was cinnamon colored from blood. We rushed over to the hospital and they flushed out my bladder and reinserted the indwelling catheter. The blood came from the inside of the bladder wall, but if we had waited much longer, I would have landed at death's door. Due to ancient technology and misinterpreted communication, we didn't immediately go back to the RIC. We stayed until the following afternoon, and even imbibed in a few beers. Not like the day before, but I don't think I cared. The catheter was doing all the work anyway. I don't remember how long it took to retrain my bladder again, but I remember I had to start all over.

As I have mentioned, sustaining a spinal cord injury like mine creates a whole slew of problems not even remotely related to the inability to move. I've often told people far and wide that the body can do things to itself far more unpleasant than pain. As warm blooded creatures, our body's temperature is regulated by an internal thermostat that keeps it warm or cool as needed, aside from extreme conditions. For many years after the accident, my temperature always ran on the cold side, but I was able to tolerate hotter temperatures, and actually liked it hot. These days, my body can't handle either. It's more of the humidity than the heat, but when it gets to the nineties and humid, I wilt like a flower! There are so many signals being sent from the brain through the spinal cord to be distributed throughout the body along a complex set of motor and sensory nerves, that I can't wrap my brain around the complexity. As I get older, and as more and more things start acting crazy in my body, my doctors really have no evidentiary answers as aging with my condition is a relatively new process, and thereby a new area of study.

After spending a total of six months in various hospitals, it was time for me to go home. I was very blessed to have a home where I could go. Snuffy was still there when I left, but I heard his parents couldn't care for him and had to institutionalize him. I never heard anything else. Having full use of his upper body, Gil was able to care for himself and moved back to the neighborhood, I think back into his parents' house. I saw him again a few times at the RIC when we had outpatient appointments at the same time. Gil was stuck. He couldn't physically work and he didn't have an education. I went home to an environment that was set up for me to prepare to go back to school. The goal was to return for the spring semester in January of 1981. The state had helped my parents with the cost of renovating their house so my wheelchair could access it. A ramp was built in the garage for easy access and one of the bathrooms was redone to accommodate my shower chair/commode. Kelly and my dad had learned how to do my personal care while my mom and my sisters, Diana and Laura, would help with just about everything else. Kelly was also getting more experience caring for me as he was going back to school with me. It would be a second chance for both of us, you might say.

My recovery and rehabilitation, and even getting to the point where I can write these words, would not have been possible without my family. I know my accident devastated them. Although he never said it, I'm sure it ruined my father's small data management business. He spent all of his time with me at the hospitals in Peoria and Chicago or on the road going back and forth. In those days, the highways were a little bit different and it took a little longer to get from Chicago to Peoria than it does now. The whole family was constantly on the move dealing with this family tragedy. My mother stayed vigilantly at my bedside and any one of my siblings would always be there also, which would allow my mom to take a break on the rare occasion when she would relinquish her post. By comparison, Gil's and Snuffy's families couldn't or wouldn't provide the same support that I had.

Diana was 22 when I was injured and she had already moved out of my parents' home and lived with some friends. I think she was 18 when she had a life-changing revelation and became a born-again Christian. She didn't like the direction her life was going and made a change in lifestyle and friends and dedicated herself to Jesus. At the time, I mocked her and her friends for being "Jesus freaks" or "Bible thumpers." I know I always believed in Jesus as far back as I can remember, but at that point in my life I had no desire to put any effort into it like attending church or being a "goody two shoes." I don't remember a whole lot about this time frame before I returned to school. Diana would visit a lot to help out. She tried many times to talk to me about Jesus, but I would have none of it.

Kelly was just about to turn 21 at the time of my fall. He was living with a friend in the vicinity of my parents' home. He really wasn't going anywhere in life in that he had dropped out of high school and was working dead-end jobs as best he could. I think he was refinishing pianos for a friend of the family who had a small piano tuning and refinishing business. We were and are as close as brothers can be, and as much as we were alike, Kelly was a bit more rebellious than me and always seemed to get in more trouble. He was and is very smart, but part of his rebellion was not doing schoolwork because that was something he was required to do. He spent a lot of time at the various hospitals and when not spending time with me, he would often go to the ER and was fascinated by the comings and goings of the ambulances and paramedics. It would have a lifelong effect on him. When I was discharged from the RIC, he moved back home to care for me and to prepare for going back to school. He would have to get his GED in order to go to college with me.

Laura was 16 in November of 1979 and was a gifted high school gymnast. I can't be certain, but I think she was hurt the most as I was her closest older brother. I had taken on the role of her protector, although she didn't need one. She was already pretty tough from being a gymnast. I made a point of making the other boys understand she could probably whup their butts by herself! I had always been mean to her when we were kids, but as a teenager I thought it was my responsibility to keep the boys away. She hated me for that! She spent a lot of time at the hospital, which affected her schoolwork and gymnastics, but she came regardless. She kept a journal of what had happened to me throughout my progress, with all the ups and downs of the struggles and triumphs I encountered. She not only chronicled what was happening with me, but how this whole thing affected my family and friends. It probably is in a box somewhere in a closet, but it would always bring a tear to my eye when I would read it. She wrote about how my friends had always regarded her as "Kevin's little sister," but by spending so much time with her and my family at the hospitals, they learned that she was so much more!

I must say, I had a pretty nice life before my accident. When I was a child, our family would move every few years due to my dad's job and I always loved moving into a new house. The unfamiliarity of the new property always presented the adventure of discovery for me. We eventually settled in Medinah where I spent most of my formative years. As a kid, I was always fast and agile and loved playing sports among many other interests. Football and hockey were my favorite sports. I was just a normal-sized kid until about eighth grade when most of the other boys hit puberty and I lagged behind. Entering high school, I stood all of five feet three inches and weighed 110 pounds dripping wet. I was trying out for the freshman high school football team and doing quite well until I got mad at the coach for disciplining me for missing practice. So I quit the team to focus on music. A few months into freshman year, I began growing. By the beginning of junior year, I was about 5' 10" but as skinny as a rail. A defining moment in my life came in gym class that year when the gym teacher had me demonstrate how to do a bench press on the universal machine. It was set at 100 pounds and I pressed it easily. Then he increased it to 115 pounds and I couldn't do it, much to my embarrassment in front of my classmates. That was it! I vowed to myself that from this point forward I would no longer be weak. I bought a weight set and protein powder to make protein shakes to help put on weight. I worked hard at it and the results started showing after a month or two. I was amazed at how quickly I was putting on muscle as I listened to Foreigner's debut album again and again in my parents' basement while I lifted weights and did sit up after sit up after sit up. That same year, the movie Rocky came out, the ultimate motivational film. That film inspired me to become something I never thought I could be. By senior year, I was one of the biggest, strongest guys in high school standing at 6' 3."

I was blessed to have such wonderful

parents as James (Jim) and Virginia (Jinny) Kindelin. My dad was an international businessman who swept my mom, a Chicago school teacher, off her feet and took her to Cali, Colombia where he worked for an American company in an American community where the American dollar went a long way. All four of us were born there, so we have dual citizenships, but we moved back to the states due to the constant insurrections and the instability of the government. We were living large in those days, but my parents realized it wasn't worth the risk. When I was hospitalized and after, they sacrificed everything to be with me. Like I said before, my father's business was virtually ruined and my mother had to take a leave from where she taught in those days in our hometown of Medinah. Without my parents, I could have ended up worse than Gil or Snuffy. One never knows, but I don't think I would have gotten to the point where I am today.

When I went home from the RIC, my father and brother assumed responsibility for my personal care, and my mother, sisters, and close friends would help out with the myriad of details, schedules, and processes it would take for me to transition into as "normal" a life as possible. Everyone was very supportive of my goal and determination to return to college in January of 1981. Some threw out the possibility that I may have been rushing it, but never discouraged me. My parents made all the arrangements with the state and university. The state counselors thought it would be better if I returned to the University of Illinois where it was more wheelchair accessible and had many more resources available to people with disabilities. I was stubborn to the point of being obstinate; I had to return to ISU. In my mind, it was the beast that knocked me down and the only way to slay that beast in return was to graduate from that institution.

Upon returning home in May of 1980, I was king of the castle. Everything revolved around me and my goal to return to school. It would seem that any family would step up in such a catastrophic circumstance, but that's not always the reality. My family was actually exceptional and tolerated me on top of the daily task of caring for me. I never felt that the world or anybody else owed me anything because of this disability, but because my family was so reliable, I came to expect their good graces, and that was wrong. I eventually got my "you know what" together, but not until I had reached the point where my Aunt Bobbie dubbed me "the tyrant on wheels." Her name was actually Mary, but when my oldest cousin couldn't pronounce that as a toddler, she became Bobbie. In later years, I asked her if I had really been that bad. She said I had my moments but it was understandable because of what I was going through.

Another wonderfully endearing effect of the spinal cord injury is low blood pressure. In these early years, I would often get dizzy and sometimes even pass out. The remedy for that was to get my head as horizontal as possible, either by lying down or leaning back in the wheelchair. There was usually someone around when something like this happened, so a remedy always came quickly and I would recover almost immediately. The exception to that rule was the one morning I passed out when I was on the toilet and left to do my business. I guess more time than usual had passed when I would usually call for help, and thus was discovered out cold. My next memory was that of being wheeled out to the ambulance, looking up and trying to ask what happened, only to have unintelligible gibberish come out. The face of Snuffy Smith flashed before my eyes when the paramedics told me I had lost consciousness. They didn't know for how long and I remember thinking I was really in trouble when very quickly the speech came back and everything seemed to be all right. I remember feeling so sorry for Snuffy. I just couldn't imagine being paralyzed *and* losing the power of speech also.

They took me to the hospital anyway to run some tests. Everything checked out fine, but I don't remember being thankful that God allowed me to dodge another bullet. I don't remember exactly, but I'm sure I gave myself all the credit for my tough guy powers of recuperation! It was so important to me to maintain the tough guy image that I think I may have even fooled myself a little bit, even though inwardly I knew I was just a little weakling.

As the months went by, I learned more and more how to function with a dysfunctional body. I continued to learn new things and got stronger. Exercise had always been important to me, so I devised new and inventive ways of improving my physical condition as best I could. I also found it necessary to come up with a "mask of false bravado" as I was terrified of what lay before me, yet I didn't want anyone to know.

Chapter 3: Back to School

In January of 1981, I jumped off the cliff and returned to ISU. It was for the spring semester, but it was actually the dead of winter. Kelly went back to school with me and was my first caregiver away from home. As he tells the story these days, my parents **told** him, in no uncertain terms, that he was going back to school with me. He likes to embellish what was his lack of education at the time as an excuse for trying to get out of that assignment, but he was willing to overcome any of his perceived shortcomings and jumped off the cliff with me. He passed the GED test without taking any preparatory classes in one attempt. So here we were, two brothers who were definitely not "normal" going to college in Normal, Illinois. As I looked out the window of our barren dorm room on that first day back, I recall feeling overwhelmed and questioned what I was doing there, but it was too late. All the arrangements had been made. Everything was put in place. People had put in a lot of work and made many sacrifices.

The campus was covered with snow and ice and the only people that were out and about were Kelly and a couple of friends who were helping us move. After we got settled, the next step was registration. I received a priority status and was able to register for any classes that I needed or I was eligible for. Kelly also received the same priority in order to work around my schedule. I decided to continue with my major of mass communication but knew I would have to make some adaptations to my goal of being a globetrotting broadcast television journalist. I couldn't take the radio or television production classes, as they were beyond my physical capability, so I focused more on writing. I regret not having worked for the campus newspaper, but I didn't think I could keep up with the pace and also didn't have much interest in being a newspaper journalist at the time. I didn't know what I wanted to do, to be honest. I learned later that I had many doubters. My goodness! I had so much self doubt; I wasn't paying attention to anybody else around me!

The mask of false bravado was up and impenetrable as I tried to work my way back into the rugby culture. A few of the older guys had graduated or just moved on, but there were still a lot of guys that I played with that were still around. My former roommates were still on campus also, but I don't remember having much contact with them at all. I don't know where the disconnect happened, but I think a lot of people were uncomfortable with my disability. It probably hit a little too close to home. One of my wildest teammates, I should say former teammates by then, asked if he could interview and photograph me for a class project. Al, I don't remember his last name, came to my dorm room with a six pack of beer and a pretty classmate named Theresa McSomething-or-other, who would take the pictures for the project. I developed an immediate crush on Theresa, and although she was very nice and friendly, she never came over to my way of thinking! I was still grappling with my self-identity. I wanted to present the tough guy image, while still allowing some vulnerability to show to some people. I didn't really want the sympathy vote, but I learned how to manipulate it. I never let go of the tough guy image, but added the intellectual know- it- all to the layers of my mask. Appearing to be smart, along with making sure everybody knew I used to be tough, was my new identity.

I quickly realized I had to meet new people and make new friends. It wasn't hard. There were people all around, especially girls! I went to one rugby match that I can remember, but didn't attend more. Even though I held onto my "I used to play rugby so therefore I'm tough" image, I knew I no longer belonged. I just felt like I was on the outside looking in. My focus had to shift. Kelly had met some girls on a different floor of our dorm and was having a debate about some topic or another. I don't remember what it was, but he asked me to come up to their room and back him up. There were two or three girls, some guy, Kelly, and me, but my attention was captured by Lynn Goscinski, a very cute sophomore with a little killer body, whom I would end up dating on and off for the next few years. The off part would be due to my own insecurities. I know now that I loved her very much but couldn't admit to it then, to her or even myself. I was afraid if our relationship went too far, she eventually would break it off with me and break my heart. Whenever it was getting to the commitment stage, I would back out.

Had I not been so insecure, I would have stayed with and eventually maybe married Lynn. She would have been perfect for me. She was smart, had a positive attitude, and looked great! I'm not sure why she even loved me. She said she did but eventually she'd had enough and didn't come back to me when I finally realized that I loved her and was willing to take a chance. She moved on and married someone else, although we remained friends for several years after college. I was even invited to, and attended, her wedding! There was another young woman I met who had a big impact on me also. Her name was Cathy Ryan. We lived in the same dorm and knew of each other but never really talked until we met at a party. I was really attracted to her, but I called it quits with her as soon as it started because of my insecurities. I know both Lynn and Cathy probably don't even remember me, but I still think about them sometimes and know that either one of them would probably have made my life a little better. I was surprised that anyone was attracted to me, but wearing the mask of false bravado allowed me to get to the point where I could even be in the relationships such as I had. To some, it may have appeared that I was very self-confident, but it was all a ruse.

Kelly and I met many new people in our dorm and classes. We hung out with the same circle of friends, for the most part. Two of the guys we met, Brent Hitchings and Bill Moeller, would become our housemates when we moved off campus after three semesters. I was desperately trying to be as "normal" as possible. Even though I felt like crawling back within myself and never having to deal with anybody or anything, I acted completely the opposite. I wanted to be where the action was! I wanted to participate in as much as I could, although it hurt to watch from the sidelines whenever there was a physical activity involved. We partied a lot and I drank a lot of beer, but I made sure I got good grades. This was Kelly's first college experience and the partying really appealed to his nature, unfortunately a little too much. He really didn't pay attention to his grades and was actually dismissed after a few semesters. He started attending Lincoln Community College in order to get his grades up and return to ISU, but he found his life's calling instead. While he was there, he took some paramedic type classes that rekindled the interest in emergency services that he had observed when I was in the hospital. There is a wonderful sidebar to the story and an example of how something good can result from a tragedy. Despite himself, Kelly was able to meet Heidy, who would eventually become his wife and stabilizing rock. He said when he saw her in the cafeteria of our dorm, he immediately knew that she was the one.

Our group would go out to parties or just hang out and listen to music or whatever. By the time we moved off campus, our younger sister Laura was attending ISU now also. One night when we were returning from a party, our housemate, Bill, was pushing my wheelchair back to our house when our group that was lagging behind called out for us to wait up. Bill and I both turned, but unknowingly came upon a curb (we were pretty sloshed too!) and I pitched forward face first out of my wheelchair into the dugout gravel of the driveway of the library that was in the process of being resurfaced. When they got me back into my chair, unbeknownst to me, one side of my face resembled hamburger meat. I just thought my nose was broken again and just wanted to get home. Everybody else tried to get me to go to the hospital but I refused. As soon as we reached the front door of our house, Laura ran inside, got a mirror and stuck it in front of my face. "Can you guys take me to the hospital?" was my reaction.

It wasn't always the circumstance that was to blame for the situations I would get myself into. Frankly, I was quite reckless. I would come flying out of my chair many times by attempting to go down inclines, hills, and ramps that I shouldn't have. I didn't care. There was always someone to pick me up. I didn't weigh all that much after losing all my muscle tone. At this point, I was just a string bean. Anyway, incidents like that were just notches in my tough guy belt. It wasn't always my fault that something bad would happen. One day, I was headed down the street in my primitively motorized wheelchair. I hated being in it and allowing it to do all the work, but it was necessary for me to be able to get to and around campus and back. The moment I would get home from classes, I would get into my manual chair. In those days, I felt like I was cheating by using the motorized chair. There were no manageable sidewalks for me to safely traverse, so I had to take the street. One day on my way to class, I noticed my neighbor sitting in his driveway with his reverse lights on. I thought he was waiting for me to pass by, but as I was crossing the entrance of his driveway, a car passed me by on my left and I realized that my neighbor was waiting for that car to pass by. I knew I wasn't going to make it, so I braced for impact as my neighbor plowed right into me. Miraculously, I was unhurt, but my chair was destroyed.

I attended classes during the summer term before the beginning of my senior year so I could make up a few of the credit hours I missed from not finishing all of the classes I was taking at the time of my fall. I thought I was dealing with a nasty summer cold, but when I was too weak to begin the fall semester, and my lips were turning blue, I finally gave in to my friends' and family's insistence that I go to the hospital. It turned out that I had pneumonia and was admitted on Tuesday afternoon. Wednesday morning, my right lung collapsed and I immediately lost consciousness requiring an emergency procedure to open it up and suck out all the fluid that had accumulated. There had been no monitors on me at that point, and had the nurse not been in the room helping me take care of my business, I would have been a goner at the ripe old age of 22! There are a few jokes there I could come up with, but I'll refrain. I spent the next three weeks in the hospital recovering. This is an example of a time when standing my ground was just being stupidly obstinate. You would think I would have learned my lesson. Stay tuned.

I caught up with my schoolwork and graduated with my classmates in May of 1983. I didn't want to participate in the graduation ceremonies, but it was important to my parents so I did it. I didn't have anything against ISU; I just wanted to get my degree and move on from there. The beast was slain. ISU really should never have been thought of as the beast in my mind at all because I was fully responsible for my actions. In essence, I was the beast.

Nevertheless, in my mind, I had won... time to go. One of the doubters that was proven wrong was the person who nominated me for outstanding Mass Communication Student, the chairman of the department. I don't remember his name, but I remember a conversation I had with him just before the end of the semester. He told me that upon observing me register for classes when I first returned, he confessed that he thought to himself that there was no way that I would be able to physically complete the program due to its journalistic requirements. He told me he thought I would never be able to keep up. I didn't win the award, and the young man who did, deserved it, but I was ecstatic and amazed at the same time that I was even nominated. I mentioned earlier how terrified I was of taking on the task of returning to school at all!

Chapter 4: Failure in the Real World

So here I was, a happy little graduate rolling his way out into the real world. In school, I didn't pursue radio or television production because of the physical limitations, but I didn't write for the school newspaper either because I didn't think I would be able to keep up. Avoidance. I used that tactic without fail on many occasions and nobody would hold me accountable. Radio and television production were out, but I think if I had written for the school newspaper, I would have been better prepared for the workforce and had more opportunities. As it were, I focused on public relations and the communications aspect of it. I applied to scores of job postings for entry-level public relations professionals. I still had my fancy typewriter from college and banged out many a cover letter. Someone or other, usually my mom or my one of my sisters, would help me fold them up with my resume and mail them out to the potential employers, hoping to get an interview. I received several replies and went on many interviews. One of my friends or my brother would get me in and out of a car, usually my mom's Oldsmobile 98, which was the biggest and roomiest, and take me to the interviews. I was all decked out in my spiffy sports jacket, tie, and slacks. I hadn't disclosed that I had a disability in any of the cover letters, and neither was it on my resume. (I hate to assign the term *disabled* to my condition because it literally means "not able.")

Unlike the college friends and teammates I knew from before my accident, the friends I'm referring to above were mostly guys I met in high school. I met Dave Polk, Nick Pasquini, and Greg Koger during our freshman year in high school. We were all in the music program, but they were all very good musicians and I was just average, as it turned out. I had forsaken football for band, realizing too late that I wasn't good enough to eventually be a professional. Dave, Nick, and

Greg, on the other hand, were exceptional on their instruments. Jeff Sauter, Tom Scott, and Dan Ward were also fellow Lake Park Lancers, but were not in the band. My barber before the accident, Jim O'Brien, became one of my close friends after. When I rolled into his shop for the first time after my fall, he seemed unfazed, but revealed in later years that he had no idea and was shocked. He said he just kept his best poker face.

After a few interviews, I could tell that I wasn't going to get the job I was applying for just by the expression on the hiring manager's face as he or she saw me sitting in the waiting room in my wheelchair. There was the awkward attempt at a handshake and a perfunctory interview, but never a call back. As the months dragged on, I continued to send out resumes and got responses but never got any second interviews. I had to use the resources around me that were available for people with disabilities to generate some kind of income. The RIC's vocational people hooked me up as a ghostwriter for Ann Landers, a famous advice columnist at the time. She was syndicated in many newspapers around the country. Her twin sister was Dear Abby who had the same type of gig. Part of her brand was that she would answer everyone who wrote in to her for advice. Everyone of those answers couldn't possibly be published in the newspaper; but everyone deserved one is what she would proclaim. It just wasn't a full-time job with benefits, and didn't pay much either as ghost writers were paid by the piece. It looked good on my resume and was a topic of conversation, but it never really paid off. I did other piecemeal type of writing work with other organizations over the years but was really getting frustrated and even depressed when no one would hire me. Discrimination was blatant as there were no laws preventing such behavior. All of the people I knew from college had full-time jobs and were pulling in decent paychecks. I felt inadequate making only a few dollars here and a few dollars there because the piecemeal work I was doing just wasn't enough to write home about. In order to make any kind of substantial income, I would have to produce a lot more pieces than I was physically capable of. I still had my trusty-old-fancy-college typewriter, but hunting and pecking with typing sticks that slipped over my paws made the going slow. Lack of full time employment led to a whole new set of feelings of inadequacy. I had been so naïve coming out of college thinking I had a fair chance at securing a good job. I was getting by on the thin government dime and the good graces of my parents. It was devastating.

I remember being pretty reckless in those days. I would come flying out of the house, down the ramp and out of the garage and onto the driveway. On a few occasions, I would hit a bump and come tumbling out of my chair. There were a couple of times when no one else was around and my mother had to call my friend Jim at his shop and ask him to come and scrape me off the driveway and put me back in my chair. He told me about one occasion when he told the customer to wait and that he would be right back to finish his haircut. I never got seriously hurt, just scrapes and bruises.

My siblings all got married in 1984 and 1985. Laura was the first. She started working in the real estate business after college and became a title examiner. She married Tom Norwood, a sheet metal worker by trade, but also the" handiest" handyman I ever met. The guy could fix or build anything! He would go on to earn his degree in later years and transitioned into other areas of his trade. We were from different worlds as far as professional interests, but we hit it off right away and became fast friends. I even attended his bachelor party, a far cry from not letting anyone near my sister! At the time, he was living in an apartment that was up a steep set of cement stairs. I wasn't too heavy to get up and down stairs in my manual chair, but it had been drizzling by the time I left and the stairs were wet. Tom, in his infinite wisdom, neglected to put his boots on before helping me down the stairs. I guess his socks slipped on the wet cement stairs and he lost control of my chair and I began the bumpy ride down. Somehow Tom managed to get in front of the chair to try to stop me from crashing to the bottom. The problem was, I probably would have flipped face first over him, most likely causing serious injury to both of us. Just at the last moment, I was able to thrust my right arm through the railing, which caught me and prevented the crash. I think this is one of those instances whereby coming out unscathed only reinforced my own misguided belief that I was some kind of invincible tough guy. Diana was also in the real estate business and eventually retired as a title officer but in 1985, she married Jonathan Kruse, a fellow Christian who was an engineer. He was very nice but I couldn't identify with him at the time. He and Diana would try to sell me on Jesus and the Bible, but I was already sold on my rowdy ways and would have none of it. I didn't disbelieve, I just didn't believe I had to put any thought into believing. In later years, Jon and I eventually became very good friends and would laugh at my past resistance. Kelly married his college sweetheart, Heidy Graber. She was already part of our crowd so she was already a friend. After I graduated, she and Kelly were living in a cheap apartment in the south suburbs. She was teaching deaf and hard of hearing students and eventually earned her Master's degree in Deafness and Rehabilitation Counseling while Kelly was beginning his career in paramedics. I know my brother will agree when I say that Heidy has been the rudder in his life who has kept him on course and probably prevented him from self-destructing. All three of my siblings raised wonderful families giving me 10 nieces and nephews along with their growing families.

I contracted pneumonia again in 1985 and had to be hospitalized for about a week. Aggressive respiratory therapy prevented it from getting as bad as it was in 1982, but I was very weakened by it and took a long time to fully recover. These were the lean years, 1983 to 1987. I spent a lot of time hanging out in Jim's shop or throwing the Frisbee in his parking lot. I had taught myself how to flip it off my thumb in an underhanded motion that wasn't half bad and usually got the Frisbee to its target. I got beaned in the face a few times when I didn't clamp my paws down quickly enough to catch it. Jim would say that he could hear and see the little birdies chirping and circling around my head. Regardless, I still wanted to play. By this time, Dave was making his living as a musician. He was in a band with a guy who was also a manager at Chicago City-Wide College. It was autumn of 1987 when Dave just happened to ask him at a band meeting if there were any jobs open that might be a good fit for me. I had gotten to know Kim McDannel by attending Dave's gigs. He was the percussionist in their band. He knew me pretty well also and said later that when Dave mentioned that I was still looking for work, a light bulb went off in his head. Kim was a manager in the Center for Disabled Student Services at the college. Most of the students he served were adults with developmental disabilities as opposed to physical ones, but the concept was the same. Why not have a person with a disability help students with disabilities? Even though I knew nothing about working with this population, he gave me a chance and hired me. He taught me all about the different theories, educational practices, and applications. Just by jumping in with both feet, so to speak, and by learning on the fly, I became knowledgeable in a whole new field where I could be of value. I was finally able to earn a regular paycheck that required me to pay taxes. I was elated! That sounds antithetical to everything Americans believe about having to pay taxes, but not being part of the workforce for so long made me feel differently. Finally, I was part of the fabric of society.

1987 was a year of mixed emotions. As

much as finally securing full-time employment was a triumph over the odds, the year had its most tragic moment when we received a call from Peggy. Leslie had passed away from some type of respiratory ailment. She was only 37 years old. Beautiful, peaceful, intelligent, and innocent Leslie had left this world to join her Creator. Yes, I believed in God Almighty at this point in my life, but as I said before, I didn't put much thought into it. I know that Leslie was a devout Catholic and had much more than a mustard seed of faith. I remember looking upon her serene face as she lay in her casket and thinking that would be me in 10 years or so, although I didn't want to be buried in a casket. I wanted to be cremated. Strange thoughts for a 27-year-old, but in those days the statistics bore out the reality that people with cervical spinal cord injuries didn't usually make it much past 40. Infections usually took over the lungs or the kidneys as time went on. As much as I was mentally prepared for an early death myself, I had no idea that in the ensuing years, I would face death on a number of occasions, yet never actually greet him.

1987 was also the year I learned how to

drive with hand controls from my wheelchair. I was on a bus on the way home from some type of therapy or medical procedure when I learned from another passenger that there were programs for people with disabilities that could teach them how to drive with hand controls and/or other necessary adaptives. I took the training, got my license, and by the spring of 1988, began the process of buying and modifying a van to fit my particular needs. It's still a complicated process today, but it was a lot worse in those days. Much of the technology was there; the practical application of it just was not that common. There was a lot of trial and error until we thought we got things right. The day after picking up the van, I was driving around my neighborhood practicing. I was supposed to pick my girlfriend up at the train station in a couple of hours and I wanted to impress her with my new driving skills. As I was taking a right turn off of the main thoroughfare, the "tri-pin" on the steering wheel that kept my hand in place locked into the tri-pin on the gas/brake hand controls which were positioned on my left against the driver's door. I struggled to unlock the tri-pins from each other, but the van kept turning right into a neighbor's front lawn and almost through the front door and window and into the living room of his ranch style home when I finally managed to jerk the tri-pins free and veered suddenly left, crashing into a couple of cars in the driveway instead. The only emotion I can remember from that incident was that of hopelessness. Losing control of a desperate situation usually doesn't elicit panic in me. Desperation and panic are two separate emotions. The owner of the house came running out, clearly infuriated until he saw that I was in a wheelchair. At this point, I felt only anger at the situation and myself, even though it was equipment failure in nature. The two cars in the driveway were pretty smashed up, but my van had only sustained a dent in the front. It was still drivable, so after the police came and issued a ticket, I proceeded to pick up my girlfriend at the train station. My mom later said she was surprised that I had the guts to drive again. At the same time I was having the dent taken out of my new van, I changed to a smaller steering wheel to avoid the same catastrophe from happening in the future.

1987 through 1993 were my "downtown Charlie Brown" years. I tried to be as much like an able-bodied person as I could. At the same time, I didn't want to be like everyone else and "rolled to the beat of my own drummer." The woman I picked up from the train station in my newly dented van was Kim Williams, a black woman from the Southside of Chicago. She worked in the registrar's office at Chicago City-Wide College and I met her when I was submitting the classes I wanted to run that term. I would also see her when I was registering my students for their classes. Interracial relationships weren't as common as they are today. Although it wasn't forbidden territory, she got a lot of flack on her end as I did on mine. We dated on and off for three years but for some reason I knew I didn't want to marry her. I wasn't insecure about this relationship and it wasn't the interracial aspect. I don't remember exactly why I broke up with her, but we remained friends for several years after that. I had a fling with a sexy Puerto Rican woman, but she didn't want to get serious. How ironic! After three years of working in the Center for

Disabled Student Services, the grant that paid my salary expired and would not be renewed. Instead of being out of a job, the position of "editor" was created for me. I had been fiddling around with their old dormant newsletter, so they were aware of my efforts and abilities and knew of my background. In my new position, I was responsible for creating, writing, editing, producing, and working with professional printers. Color printing from computers was very expensive in those days so big jobs were sent out. Even though it didn't pay much, it was a dream job for me! The people responsible for keeping me employed were Martha Bazik, the president of the college at the time, Dick Humphries, executive dean of faculty and staff development, and John Wozniak, dean of adult education.

I can't remember the exact year, but it was either the summer of 1991 or 92, when I learned how to fly... Unfortunately, it was only for a short distance over a ditch! I arrived at Nick's family's old Victorian style house where he was living again after a brief stint playing drums in a rock 'n roll band in California. It wasn't cutting it, so he also took a job on the lower rungs of the corporate ladder. That whole atmosphere intimidated him to the point where he came back to the Chicago area to stay in his boyhood home in Itasca. It's a beautiful neighborhood and the house is now a landmark but no longer with the family. Regardless, I would often drive over there in my big, midnight blue, full-sized van. I had all the windows except the driver's and passenger's, tinted limousine black so no one could see in. I loved my E150! It guzzled a lot of gas, but it took me everywhere. I pulled into his driveway that evening and determined that the slope was too steep if I were to roll out in the manual chair I was still using in those days. I had done that many times before and sometimes ended up in the grass due to that slope. I pulled out of the driveway on the corner lot and parked on the side of the street of his house. I judged the incline to be less severe, so I opened the doors and unfolded the platform that would let me down to the ground. At the end of the platform was a short barrier that unfolded when the platform reached the ground to allow me to get off of it. It was designed to stop the wheelchair from rolling off while it was in the upright position. It did its job when I rolled out onto the platform way too quickly and realized too late that where I parked was still too severe to prevent me from hitting the end of the platform and launching over the ditch and onto the sidewalk. The chair stayed on the platform, but I was a crumpled mess on the sidewalk. Nick, one of his brothers, and his sister Maria ran over to help me back in the chair and assess the damage. My elbow and face were pretty skinned up and the severe pain in my left wrist turned out to be a broken bone, but in the meantime, Maria was attending to my wounds. She was three or four years older and I always had a crush on her and now she was a nurse cleansing and dressing my wounds! We laughed and joked around a bit and then after a few beers and conversation, I went home. The next day, my wrist hurt way too much so I got a ride over to the ER because it was too painful to drive myself. A bone at the base of where the index finger meets the thumb, called the scaphoid, had snapped and popped out of place. Surgery was the normal course of action to put the little piece that was floating around in there back in place. The doctor wasn't sure what to do because he had never done surgery on a quadriplegic hand. He said he wanted to consult with some hand specialists before proceeding and just re-casted me for the time being. In the meantime, I still had to get around. Now that the cast was too wide for me to put my hand into the tri-pin that controlled the gas and brake, I had to come up with a solution. My friend, Greg, has always been mechanically inclined. He did a temporary re-engineering job by simply widening the space between the two tri-pins where my wrist went with a piece of metal that functioned as an extender. I just wedged my cast in there, fashioning it so that it would only come out if I lifted up. Nobody said it wasn't legal! A guy has to get around! The next time I saw the doctor, he said that the hand specialists didn't have any advice for him so we just had to go in to see what was what. As he was examining my most recent x-rays, he turned to me in a very surprised manner and asked me what I had done. He explained that the scaphoid had popped back into place on its own. He said the only way he could think of to accomplish what he called a self-reduction was to squeeze the hand into a fist. It's usually much too painful to bear and I couldn't do it anyway. I thought about it and remembered having painful hand spasms recently that I couldn't stop that must have done the job. Case closed. Just a few more weeks of dealing with a cast and I would be good to go! To quote the song, "I get knocked down, but I get up again."

1993 was the year I lost my job and gained a wife. Chicago City-Wide College was one of eight colleges in the Chicago City College system. The powers that be decided to shut it down and funnel some of its programs into one or more of the other colleges. I guess if you don't have a school, you don't need someone to write about it and promote its programs and people. I was out. John Morrow was the director of resource development at the time and his office was right across from my desk area. I wasn't quite important enough to get an office, but my area looked out the window and was pretty nice. John hired me on under a grant he was working with and we all moved to Harold Washington College. It was only temporary, but the thought was it would buy me time to find another editor type position. John also said he thought it would be a good idea for me to get something published in a major periodical. He said he knew a guy who could get me published in the Chicago Sun-Times if I wrote about something contemporary and it was actually worth publishing. I wrote an op-ed piece about my disdain for the politically correct language of the day, particularly regarding people with disabilities and other conditions. I basically argued that assigning labels that society might feel comfortable with, but are inaccurate, is an excuse to dance around the truth.

Chapter 5: Marriage and Divorce

To say Maggie changed my life would be an understatement. I met her when she literally walked through my front door, okay it was my parents' front door. I was still living with them in 1993. I didn't have the means in many ways to live on my own. She came to apply for the caregiver job. She was very young at 18 and was visiting the U.S. on a visa from Poland. I hired her and thought she was very attractive. Her name was Malgorzata, or Margaret in English. She went by Maggie with Americans and Gosia with her Polish relatives. I quickly became more than infatuated, and despite the age difference, I wanted to ask her out on a date. It was very easy to talk with her and she exhibited a unique intelligence that I was especially attracted to. She was young and hot and why would she want to go out with an older crippled guy? At this point in my life, I was pretty bold so I asked her out anyway and she said yes. I was able to able to take her to a fancy place in town because my parents charged me very minimal rent, even for those days. She was impressed and one thing led to another and she became not only my caregiver, but my girlfriend. I fell head over wheels in love and spent as much time as I possibly could with her. We had a great time doing everything together from dining out to doctors' appointments. Yes, even doctors' appointments were more tolerable when she was along. When we were driving, we would sing songs that came on the radio, many times with our own lyrics! It was just a joy to be around her. Ours was not a traditional courtship. From that first date forward, we were unofficially a couple. Due to the inconsistency of caregiving, she was with me almost 24/7. I quickly realized that her visa would soon be up and she would have to return to Poland. She wouldn't be eligible to return again for another five years and that would pretty much be that for any kind of relationship. I decided to ask her to marry me.

She was ecstatic at first and said yes, but then soon realized the gravity of marrying me. The 14-year age difference was only an issue with some of her relatives, not including her mother, who still lived in Poland. Becoming the wife of a man with as much baggage to carry as me was a daunting commitment indeed! Maggie's mother didn't speak a lick of English, but through our translated conversations with her daughter as translator, she apparently really liked me. I liked her also. Maggie turned to her for advice because she didn't know what to do. She lived with her uncle who was a permanent resident and married. Tom was a little leery of me at first, but clearly came to like me a lot also. It took a lot longer to convince her aunt Sofie! Maggie told me that her mother asked her one simple question.... "Do you love him?" Maggie said yes, so her mother told her to stay and marry me. This was significant because they were especially close. Maggie's father had been killed in an accident when she was just six years old.

I'm glad her mom, Barbara, or Basia in Polish, was on my side! I was wise enough to know that it was going to be a bureaucratic nightmare to make everything legal. Immigration and Naturalization Services (INS) interviewed us to determine if this was a marriage of convenience or the real deal. I guess we convinced them because they approved the papers! As we were getting off the elevator at one of the downtown buildings, the elevator car didn't come up level with the floor, so I pitched forward and had one of those "face to floor" moments again. The bigger problem was the heavy elevator doors closing on my ankle and breaking it. There was definitely some pain involved, but it was worth the settlement money the building owner paid out. I had never thought about those things, but after I was lifted back into my chair by my soon-to-be bride and a witness or two, we finished our business and I was advised by our immigration lawyer that I had a case against the building owner. Of course I tried to play it off as nothing because I was the tough guy! I remember being sternly advised that this was not the time to be the tough guy. I was never really a fan of profiting off of breaking my bones, but the money helped out with the beginning of a marriage.

Two or three weeks before the wedding was scheduled for June 12, I contracted a dreaded urinary tract infection, commonly known as a UTI. Most women know what I'm talking about due to anatomy and most men have no clue, but due to compromised immune systems, spinal-cord injured men are typically very susceptible. This was a particularly nasty one, but I still managed to get by during its early stages. Headaches, muscle aches, increased spasms are clear indicators of worse things yet to come. The infection could take over and shut down the bladder from being able to void. At this point, hyper-reflexia occurs where everything just goes haywire! The blood pressure spikes and a stroke can occur. I mentioned hyper-reflexia in an earlier chapter describing how I unwittingly almost killed myself by drinking too much beer. Catheterization is required to release the pressure from the malfunctioning bladder. It could eventually blow up like a balloon and burst, usually killing the person. I didn't want to have to deal with any of that so I went to a doctor I didn't really know all that well, just hoping to get some antibiotics and get it taken care of quickly. He prescribed antibiotics that turned out to have terrible side effects.

The first of the horrible side effects I can recall from this antibiotic occurred on the night I was going to join my pals for my bachelor party. I was in the bathroom brushing my teeth or hair or something, when the lights went out! I couldn't see anything. I was blind! After another quick trip to the ER, I immediately stopped taking that medicine, but my vision would fade in and out for the next few days, including the day of my wedding. Up until just a few days before the wedding, I was having the most horrific headaches I ever experienced. It felt like a jack hammer was going off inside my head and I think that's what migraine sufferers must deal with. The combination of the pounding headaches and the overall weakness I felt was more than debilitating. We postponed our little honeymoon for a week, but it took 3 ½ hours to drive the normal 1 ½ hour drive to a resort in Wisconsin when we finally did go. I could see by then, but I had to continually pull over due to weakness.

With the help of Aunt Bobbie who found the article about decent, accessible housing in the area, we found a nice little one-bedroom place we could rent from the Northwest Independent Living Association (NWILA), which bought and rehabbed six units in a condominium building in Palatine, a suburb only 13 miles from my boyhood home in Medinah. I had not yet secured another editorial position, but being married, I took a job with the credit card wing of a Chicago bank. It was eventually eaten up by one of the larger "big banks." Because I don't want to besmirch anyone's reputation unnecessarily, I won't name the company I worked for but I will say it was the worst job I ever had! My job was in dispute resolutions and customers would call in screaming and hollering even though we were there to help them. For the most part, they didn't realize that their dispute was with the merchant and we were on their side. After a few years and a couple of disappointments where I didn't get promotions I was sure I deserved, I ended up just dealing with customer correspondence. I still had to fix mostly greedy people's problems, but at least I didn't have to hear them screaming at me!

Diving 23 miles to Elgin and back was my new daily routine by early 1994. Maggie was going to college at Harper Community College in Palatine and was working part-time as best she could. I hated my job but I loved my wife and wanted to do the best I could to provide for her. Upon completion of my long journey home, she would typically have a cup of coffee waiting for me, except when we were arguing of course, which wasn't all that much. She would help me get out of my chair to get some pressure relief, and then back into it after about an hour. There were leverage techniques for transferring, but I know it hurt her back. We would have an aide in the morning to do the early routine, but if she didn't show, Maggie would do the work. At first it wasn't that much of a problem, but eventually it would take its toll.

On one hot July evening in 1994, I fell asleep at the wheel driving home from Elgin. A decade later I was diagnosed with sleep apnea, but I'm not sure if I can blame the accident on that. My big, midnight blue Ford E150 drifted into the next lane, collided with another car, and spun out of control, smashing into the ditch. I came to a stop upright on the wheels but I must have rolled because the top was crushed. A little background is required here to give a full explanation. I always tried to keep in the best shape possible and devised different ways to achieve that. When I lived with my parents, I had a heavy bag, the kind boxers train on, hanging in their garage. I would go out every evening and pound the snot out of it. Okay, so heavy bags don't have snot, but they don't have the other word I was thinking of either! I would also drive out to Busse Woods forest preserve that had a bicycle track that went all around the preserve. I would get on it with my manual chair and push to my heart's content. Not too long before this most recent debacle, I switched from my standard, clunky wheelchair to a sleek chair made in Sweden. It was lightweight and streamlined, allowing me to propel my chair more efficiently and easily around the track and everywhere else. With this switch, along with my other exercises, I developed into about as good a conditioned quadriplegic man one could be. This also impacted my driving situation. The

H-bar that was bracketed to the wheelchair that held the bolt that locked me into the lockdown device which was bolted to the floor of my van, had to be fitted to my new wheelchair. The problem was, it wasn't a perfect fit because the Swedish chair was metric as opposed to the standard fittings of my previous chair. The company that modified the van basically had to put a square peg into a round hole but was able to secure the H-bar. The chair stayed in place under normal driving circumstances, but not when I crashed at 70 mph. I bounced around like a ping-pong ball and ended up with my head at the gas and brake pedals facing up. Blood was streaming down my face and I could hear the engine whining and smell the fire underneath my van. I remember thinking that I was glad I had life insurance and that Maggie would be okay. For some reason, I reached up to try to turn off the engine, only to see the pinky of my left hand just dangling there. Just when I thought the van was going to blow, the door suddenly slid open and a woman who identified herself as an off-duty paramedic stabilized me. She said she had witnessed the accident and pulled over to help. She told me another off-duty paramedic who was not with her was putting out the fire. Back then, I just chalked it up to coincidence. These days, I don't believe there are any coincidences in God's world.

I was pretty messed up, to say the least. The surgeon who put me back together estimated that my right femur had shattered into 25 pieces. He understatingly categorized it as a "high energy fracture." Piecing it all together with titanium plates, screws, and wires, x-rays revealed an amazing piece of work. He reattached my left pinky and stuck a few pins through it, holding it to my hand. It was useless then as it is now anyway, but it looks better with it on. My forehead had bounced off the windshield and left a little chunk in it. I have a nice scar that bears witness to this day. Worst of all, I was laid up in the hospital for several weeks and unable to work. I had not yet met the six-month mark to qualify for short-term disability pay, and therefore had no income. Maggie had a part-time job at the college but that wasn't going to pay the rent. We were in trouble. Outwardly, I was trying to show a brave face that I would soon recover from this latest catastrophe and everything would be all right, but inwardly I was feeling lost and more than scared. I was helpless.

In a vain attempt to save a little money, I had dropped the comprehensive insurance coverage on my van, just keeping the required liability. My only option now was to sell the salvageable parts off of the totaled vehicle. My parents let me keep it in their driveway while I was doing that, but my mom made us put a tarp over it because that chunk of flesh from my forehead was still in the windshield! I made a few dollars by selling some of the parts, but it didn't help much. I was hospitalized for several weeks but somehow was able to apply for and receive food stamps. Maggie was so ashamed of using the food stamps, so Aunt Bobbie stepped up and exchanged them for cash. She wasn't ashamed to use them in a grocery store line. Maggie was trying so hard to play the role of the good wife and using food stamps didn't fit with her image of that, I guess. Aunt Bobbie also stepped up with $1000 in cash. After several weeks, I don't remember exactly how many, I was released from the hospital. My surgically repaired leg had a very restrictive brace that kept it immobile. It was a little bit too much for Maggie to manage, so we moved in with my parents while I healed. They even gave us the master bedroom because it was closer to the master bathroom with the roll in shower. When I lived there before I got married, I stayed in a bedroom across the hall, which worked just fine. I'm just very fortunate and blessed to have had such considerate parents. Nevertheless, all of this put a strain on our marriage. We were pretty much broke. We couldn't go anywhere until my leg could bend, and when it did we had to get in and out of her car, which was very difficult for her. Eventually, we got through it. I went back to work and saved up for another van while Maggie continued working on her degree. We moved back to our own place and tried to start anew. It took several months for the jigsaw puzzle of my leg to fully heal, but at this point, I didn't have my own transportation. I was able to utilize a service provided by the many interrelated companies and government authorities involved. A minivan would pick me up at home and take me to work and back. It was a great service for getting me to and from work but was limited to a certain "corridor" along the train lines and usually it didn't take us where we wanted to go in our social life. We had to resort to getting in and out of her car, which of course put more wear and tear on her back.

It was the day after Mother's Day in 1996 when my father lost his battle with cancer. Cancer of the larynx had only been diagnosed about a year earlier. My father was the nicest guy you could ever meet, but he was also the toughest son of a gun I ever knew. He endured several surgeries, chemotherapy, and radiation therapy in order to keep working as a businessman. After they removed his larynx, he had to learn a new way of talking and swallowing. Throughout my whole life I never heard him complain about pain of any kind until a few months before he died when he told me he had never known what it meant to "hurt down to the bone," but now he knew. This was a devastating loss for me. Most importantly, he was my dad. We had a great relationship before my accident, but he became even more instrumental in my life after it by being there for me and also showing me so many of the ins and outs of life. I didn't know anything about being an adult before my accident. I was so fortunate to have my parents teach me how to grow up. I may not have done such a great job in doing so, but my parents more than made up for my inadequacies as I slowly learned. It would be a couple of years before I realized the full impact of losing my father.

Finally, by the spring of 1997, we had saved up enough to make a down payment on another van that would make monthly payments affordable. A lot of work and specialized equipment would go into modifying one of these vans. A person just doesn't waltz into a dealership showroom and waltz right out with a vehicle equipped with the specialized equipment that I would need. I won't bore the reader with the detailed specifics of making all the ends meet in order to get a finalized product. I bought another Ford E150. The body style was a little different on this emerald green 1996 model than the 1987 one. The equipment and modifications I used were basically the same except for some minor differences or updates. The engine was a lot more powerful though. That was my favorite van, other than the one I'm driving these days. I was so happy to be free again! Maggie's back was happy too, but the damage was already done. Things were not bad though. In fact, things were good. We could go places. She was able to finish her degree and start work as an accountant. Around this time, we were informed that the organization that owned our apartment, the Northwest Independent Living Association (NWILA), was going bankrupt. We had the option of buying the one-bedroom condo or moving out. There wasn't a lot of good accessible housing in the Chicago area, and we really didn't want to take on the burden of trying to find a place with all that was going on in our lives. We decided to buy, but at the last moment, the 2- bedroom balcony unit occupied by the now deceased president of the NWILA and his wife became available. She didn't have a disability and felt that she shouldn't still live there and asked if I wanted to buy it. There were a few other people who decided to buy their units also. There was just one problem. There was no one to buy them from. The president of the organization had recently passed away and his wife did not want to assume those responsibilities. In order to sell the various units to the prospective buyers, a board had to be created. I was elected president so that someone could sign off on the papers and make it official. Just like that, Maggie and I were homeowners.

There was definitely love in this marriage, but I think the seeds were sown somewhere along the path that she wanted to do something else with her life other than be saddled with the baggage that came with being married to me. It came out of left field. I never saw the signs. She said she wanted a divorce and it hit me like a sucker punch. Sorry for the mixed metaphors, but I wanted to emphasize the impact I felt from this announcement. I had been riding high in life, despite having a disability. I had overcome a lot of obstacles to get where I was. I earned my degree despite the naysayers. I managed to secure gainful employment despite the blatant discrimination that was prevalent in those days. I had a beautiful wife. We lived a modest life but I thought we had a happy little marriage. I was wrong.

I realized that the age difference wasn't the issue; Maggie just didn't want to live life as my wife and backup caregiver. I think she would've been happy to just be my wife. Working, doing all the physical work of caring for the household, caring for me in one way or another was all just too much for her. Years later, she said she may not have divorced me if my father hadn't passed away at that time. He was very helpful to her with the things I couldn't do that needed a man's touch. Not that a woman can't do those things, it's just that Maggie was so inexperienced. It was also that she was still very young and wanted to do other things with her life. As it were, she just wanted out. She never gave me the exact reason, just the old "I'm not happy" excuse. She said she still loved me and wanted to remain "best of friends" but couldn't stay married to me and had to move out. It was 1998 that she moved into an apartment in Chicago. We still kept our finances together and I held on to the hope that she would come back to me. We still enjoyed each other's company but not as man and wife. I also noticed that she enjoyed the company of younger friends from where she worked and lived. As the rock band, The Eagles would say, she was already gone.

As I mentioned earlier, I had been riding

pretty high in life despite the disability. Sure, my daily routine was still very difficult and I couldn't do things I did before, but I had love and security. Then suddenly, these were taken away from me. The very thing I so feared from the days I returned to college up until I married Maggie actually happened. My self-fulfilling prophecy came true. The one I finally committed to left me because of my disability. It crushed me and sent me in a downward spiral for the next few years. We still did things together for a while and she would come over to do bills or deal with other financial matters. She was beginning to meet a whole new set of friends, leaving me to my own devices on many an occasion. As much as she tried to help me with finding and training caregivers that would be "live in," the quality of my care really took a nosedive. The pay wasn't all that great in those days resulting in a revolving door of people. On occasion, Maggie would come back and help, but that was only temporary. This rejection devastated me even more than how I felt from the original accident. I don't know why, but mentally I had been able to bear the consequences and effects of my spinal cord injury better than how I felt and still feel from having love disappear from my life. I think that because I always had to focus on an objective in order to function with my disability, I never let the mental aspect of it drag me into the abyss, even though I get down all the time from it. Having someone whom I loved dearly take away the love she pledged would last forever just ripped a hole in me that never fully healed. I won't go into all the stupid things I did in pursuit of love and affection, but in the years from 1998 to 2000 I was doing exactly what the old country song accused me of... I was looking for love in all the wrong places. I was desperately lonely so I began hanging out with people I normally wouldn't have, just for the company. They were just people who lived in the building and were around to have a few drinks with. I don't mean to judge them in any way; it's just that we were from different worlds and I didn't have much in common with them other than a desire to numb whatever pain there was. As much as I hoped, I knew in my heart that Maggie was not going to come back to me. She came back a few times to help with the caregiving, but no romance came with the deal. Not only did she break my heart, but she put back upon me all the responsibility I had become accustomed to sharing. I felt more secure in making decisions with a partner. Now I was on my own and it was a very lonely feeling. To say Maggie would change my life is an understatement, for better and for worse. Still, life goes on and I had to keep trying.

Chapter 6: Getting Worse before Getting Better

For the two years we were separated, I clung to the hope of reconciliation and tried to get Maggie to go to marriage counseling, but she didn't want to get back together and said there was no need for counseling. The divorce was eventually finalized in 2000 and that was that for my days spent in wedded bliss. We remained friendly and I kept the place as it was equipped for my special needs. Moving forward, I would always need to have a live in caregiver, which would prove to be more difficult than I ever imagined. The money wasn't all that great in those years and people would come and go. This lack of consistency always made me anxious. I recall having a multitude of health issues for several years, usually infections or other conditions that may have come with inadequate care. I can't blame it all on bad caregiving. I was pretty self-destructive also. In early 1999, I came down with walking (rolling) pneumonia. I was feeling run down and congested for quite a while before I relented and went to the doctor. Upon examination, he revealed that I looked like bleep. Okay, so he said another word for bleep but I'm trying to keep this book PG, despite having a sometimes R-rated life! He prescribed the right antibiotics which eventually cleared it up and I kept going on my merry way. Actually, I was miserable. My wife had left me. I hated my job. I was anxious due to the instability in my life. What could be worse? One of the heaviest snowfalls in Chicago history fell upon us that month, around 20 inches. I was driving home from work on the tollway one evening when I saw a car pass on my right going much faster than conditions allowed. A few seconds later, I was staring at his headlights after he had spun around in the snow. We collided head on, which launched my van over the median, landing on the passenger side. My chair remained locked to the device bolted to the floor, no bouncing around like a ping-pong ball this time! My

van was totaled but I was unhurt. My poor
Van! My V8 5.4 litre Triton, emerald green
Ford E150 met its demise due to no fault of
my own. It turned out that the guy who hit me
was a doctor who worked at the hospital I was
taken to as a precaution. But he didn't even
stop in to apologize when they were checking
me out.

I was without a vehicle again, but this time
the other person's insurance was going to pay
to replace it and also agreed to provide
transportation to and from work. Still, the
process of buying and building a van to meet
my specific needs would take several months.
If you noticed a pattern in buying Ford E150s,
it was because they were most suitable for
modifying in those days. I think my next one
was model year 2000, which looked exactly
the same as the 1996. I just hoped I would
never have to test the aerodynamics of flying
over the median wall on this one, but it
wouldn't fare much better in the end. It was
dark blue, not as cool as my original midnight
blue vehicle, but still cool. It had a V8 4.6 litre
Triton engine that was pretty fast for its size,
but not like the 1996. During the building
process of the 2000, I had the misfortune of

being involved in another traffic accident as a passenger. I was being transported in a modified van to the builder to make adjustments and fittings. Quite suddenly and without warning, as most accidents tend to be, a vehicle pulled out right in front of us attempting to make a left turn through heavy traffic. It was a catering truck, so it provided a nice wall for us to slam into. I guess my head bounced off the top of the windshield frame because I ended up with dark "raccoon eyes." Everything else checked out okay in the hospital but I acquired a new, mostly inexplicable, pain on my right side. It felt like someone had smashed me in the ribs with a baseball bat, but scans revealed no damage. It was determined to be neurological damage around the original fusion site that sent pain signals to my right side, and only my right side. My doctor prescribed a neurological medication that I use to this day. After everything was said and done, I had another new van ready to take me on my adventures.

It was during this time that I was interviewing for a caregiver when a very attractive nurse from Philippines interviewed for the job. She ended up not taking it because the pay was low, but there was a palpable attraction between the two of us. We ended up dating and entering into a relationship that negatively impacted my life for several years. I don't want to give her the dignity of recognition by talking too much about her or the relationship. I will just say that she was an opportunist that took advantage of the situation and especially my dependency on other humans for basic needs.

It was by 2000 that my muscle spasms had gotten out of control. There was nothing that could completely stop them. Without warning, I would feel a major spasm run up my back and abdomen that would lift me out of my chair and sometimes onto the floor if I didn't catch myself in time or if it were too powerful. By December of that year, I had surgery to implant an intrathecal pump in my abdomen that would deliver the medicine directly to my spine. In the ensuing years, it actually ruined my muscle tone throughout the rest of my body, but it was necessary for me to be able to function.

I was still working for the credit card company and really felt like my life was in a rut. I was able to write a few freelance articles for a local newspaper, The Daily Herald, with the thought that they would increase my portfolio, hopefully giving me a better chance to secure a full-time writing position again. They were human interest articles. One was about a barbershop quartet comprised of four gentlemen all older than 65, and the other featured a father-son bagpipe duo. They were a lot of fun to do, but with my full-time work schedule, the amount of time and effort it took to interview the subjects, listening to the recordings back and forth in order to write my articles, it was just not worth what I was getting back, which was about 150 bucks per article and no new writing positions. Aside from that, I hate the sound of the bagpipes. That might sound sacrilegious coming from someone who has mostly Celtic DNA, but the nasally whine that emits from them doesn't strike me as pleasant. I hope all of you bagpipe-playing readers don't hate me for this!

It felt like I was spinning my wheels in that rut I just mentioned, metaphorically speaking this time. I had to make a change so I applied for executive advisor, a lower-level management position where I worked. The job entailed taking on the very difficult situations and especially angry customers. Soon after, a position which clearly aligned with my talents and abilities was created. It was a kind of communications liaison that would develop, write, and present information to help facilitate better lines of internal communication structures. I interviewed for the position and everything went very well. Everybody thought I was a slam-dunk to be hired, including the manager who was hiring for the executive advisor position. He told me he was going to hire one of the other candidates even though he thought I was the best who had applied because he was certain I would be offered this new position. It was supposed to be a "site-specific" position for the Elgin, Illinois branch where I worked but the hiring manager was in Columbus, Ohio and decided to hire someone she was familiar with from that location. This was another severe blow and I wondered how many more catastrophes and disappointments I would have in life. I think I was actually wondering if I was being tested. Was God testing me? Was the devil trying to get to me? Why did I have such bad luck? Why did I have to keep getting back up from getting knocked down? I was getting sick of hearing the Chumbawamba song in my head again and again!

Because this latest disappointment was foremost in my mind, I wasn't focused on the drive to work the next morning and took my hand out of the tri-pin of the steering wheel to adjust the heat at 70 mph on the tollway. The van hit a bump and veered immediately into the median wall. No flying over it this time, just smack dab right into it. The van was totaled and I was in the ER once again. My mother and the person I was dating met me at the hospital and were present when the doctor announced I was about half an hour away from cardiac arrest from internal bleeding due to a lacerated liver. The tri-pin on the steering wheel jammed into the pump in my abdomen, tearing into and lacerating the liver. They were pumping blood into me in an attempt to stop the internal bleeding and avoid surgery. He said if I had to have surgery I only had a 50% chance of getting off the table. Their attempts were successful of course, but I had to be hospitalized for a week, the first few days in the ICU hooked up to all kinds of machines. The pain I felt from this injury was the worst I can ever remember, and that's saying quite a bit. The day after I returned home, I experienced a severe burning sensation in my stomach and began vomiting blood. I had to return to the ER where they pumped my stomach and put me on medication to heal the esophageal reflux damage that had occurred due to being hooked up to the machines. Lucky me! At least I didn't have to be hospitalized again.

Once again, I was without my own transportation. I used the insurance money for a down payment for another Ford E150. Any insurance claim is based upon the depreciated value of the vehicle, so it was like starting over each time, no matter how close I was to paying off the previous van. I had to resort to using the rail corridor program to get me from home to work and back again. It wasn't really a good option for social occasions, so my personal life was rather limited for the next several months. This van was a silver 2001 model and the least favorite of all of my vehicles. The modifier I chose was not my best choice as a lot of ongoing issues arose with the vehicle long after it was built and I was driving it. At least I could get around again, even if it wasn't a vehicle without problems. My previous three vehicles all had their unique characteristics that I enjoyed, but this one was just plain old transportation to get me from here to there.

Over all the years, the bane of my functional existence has been pressure sores. Sitting up long hours working, even just sitting in a bad position, can cause pressure sores. Aside from staying off of one's bottom, there is no way to prevent them completely. The only thing that could be done was to get off of them as much as possible to heal them as quickly as possible. Of course, that would interrupt work and would usually lead to an extended absence that had financial implications. It was during these times that I got the most anxious and depressed about things that were out of my control. Being stuck in bed is not my idea of relaxing. Even now, whenever I have to lie on my belly for any amount of extended time, I get depressed but I focus on the knowledge that there is an end in sight and eventually I will be up and about. The only thing I *can* do in these circumstances is to not give up.

In late 2002, I fell asleep at the wheel on the way to work. The front end of my silver beast ended up in the back end of a semi. Again, my van was totaled but I thought I was okay. When I unlocked from the lockdown box I saw a six-inch gash on the inside of my knee that was eventually stapled shut in the ER. Child's play, ha! I had been falling asleep in meetings at work and sometimes even at my desk. I knew there had to be something wrong so I gave in and saw my doctor and was diagnosed with sleep apnea. As soon as I started wearing that incredibly uncomfortable CPAP mask, I never had an accident again. That was actually my last one and I've been getting a safe driver discount for any of those who may have been snickering at my driving record! The last full-size van I purchased and drove was a 2003, wait for it... Ford E150. This time around, the process was completely different. I didn't have to go to a Ford dealer and then bring a standard conversion van to a modifier to tear apart, rebuild, and customize to my specific needs. It still all had to be certified by a licensed qualified individual before any modifier would do any work. Liability can rear its ugly head! The difference here was the van and modifications were all done in the same place so the process was much smoother and less time-consuming. It still took a few months, but in the end it was a better product and lasted a total of 12 years until I traded it in on the 2014 – Dodge Grand Caravan that drives like a dream and I still drive now. I bought it in 2015 as a pre-driven vehicle and it's still going strong today! I must admit; I am now a Mopar convert. You were right all along Tom Norwood.

It was during these years that I finally realized I had to do something different than just persevere. It was in my nature to be stubborn and never give up, but it hit me that I couldn't do it alone. I didn't consider the person who had attached herself to me like a parasite as my partner, so I truly felt all alone. By 2005, the intrathecal pump implanted in my body had taken its toll. The sacrifice for controlling the previously almost uncontrollable muscle spasms was muscle tone. The muscles that used to spasm had maintained their definition as a result, but when the discomfort became dangerous, they had to be quieted. Consequently, my body turned to mush and by that time I not only required a power wheelchair to get around, but I needed it more for the ability to lean and tilt the chair as needed for pressure relief. Pressure sores had become a big problem and routinely knocked me out of commission over the years for extended periods of time.

Chapter 7: Growing in the Faith

Finally, the mustard seed planted deep inside me long ago began to grow, or maybe I just allowed it to grow. That's the only thing I did differently. It wasn't a sudden epiphany or revelation, but a gradual opening up to the Lord's will instead of following my own. It took me until 2005 to seek out a church where I could worship and learn about Jesus. Dave and I went to check out this nondenominational mega-church in my town to see if that was something we might like. It wasn't, and I didn't feel like I fit in. It was more like a bunch of young Christians checking each other out, and besides that, the pastor seemed to contradict himself within his own message. That's all I'll say about them. Dave said he knew someone who attended a Lutheran Church that was just down the street from me.

I wasn't concerned with the denomination. I just wanted to pursue my Christianity.

I began attending Immanuel Lutheran Church in Palatine in 2005. I also lost my job with the bank that year. I had been out for an extended period of time with a pressure sore. This was the sore that was the last straw and drove me to go from my manual chair to a power chair that would allow for better pressure relief. I don't remember exactly when I went out on leave, but I remember it was September when I called them to let them know I was healed and ready to return. I was informed that I had exhausted my protected leave and was released from my position. I could interview for other positions within the corporation, but if I didn't find something, I would no longer be an employee after 60 days. How nice! I immediately started applying and interviewing for other jobs. It didn't take too long to get a few interviews due to the immediacy of the internet and the ability to search and apply for a much greater number of positions. Now in the days of the information superhighway (that's what it used to be called when the internet first became a reality), prospective employers can also be on the internet prowl, and that's how my most current employer found me. With all of this going on in my life, I started feeling I was going in the wrong direction with my personal life in pursuit of emotional satisfaction and happiness. After checking out the mega-church, I started going to Immanuel, a medium-sized Lutheran church precisely one mile from where I live. It was strange going to a place where I didn't know anybody and voluntarily going to the kind of place my parents had to drag me to in the past. I didn't know how people would react to me. I assumed they would be nice because I always thought Christians were supposed to be nice, but I also felt they wouldn't be wrong to judge me. I'm not sure I even knew what I was looking for at this point. I only knew that I wanted to connect to the God I had learned about as a boy. I remember Him being gracious and forgiving, as well as having all the answers. I knew I wasn't always going to **hear** all the answers, but I was hopeful He was listening.

At first, I would just zip inn, listen to the service, and zip right back out. It took me a little while before I started fellowshipping with other people. I had no idea at first who provided them, but there were always snacks and coffee available between and after services. I don't think I would qualify as the shy type, but I don't really go out of my way to talk to people out of my comfort zone. I knew a little bit about the Bible, as I mentioned from my previous upbringing, but I also had read it a few years earlier. When I expressed an inkling of curiosity about Jesus around my sister Diana and Jonathan, I received a copy of the Good News Bible soon after for Christmas. I didn't feel like I knew enough about it to engage in conversations with people who had been churchgoers for all or most of their lives. Regardless, I put on my mask, put my insecurities aside, and began to meet people. I remember meeting Wendy Maulding in Fellowship Hall, snacking on coffee cake and sipping coffee. I don't remember the conversation except that she said I needed to meet her husband John, and that he was coming down from Bible study. The church also had a school and he was coming from a Bible study that was using one of the empty classrooms on a Sunday. John was a very charismatic, gregarious person who was easy to like. He was also easy to dislike because he was a man of his convictions and couldn't get pushed around. He was open to different opinions, but you couldn't force yours on him. We hit it off right away and became fast friends. I really enjoyed going to church every Sunday, worshiping, learning, and fellowshipping, but I still didn't know my place. This was all new territory to me.

One Sunday, John said I should join them in Bible study upstairs. This was problematic because it was right during the middle service, which was the one I attended and was most convenient for me. I hemmed and hawed, as my mother would say, for several weeks until I finally relented. I decided I could stick around and attend the later service, which was contemporary and had a praise band. I didn't really want to get up any earlier to attend the first service, which was traditional with all the hymns that I wasn't really into. The Bible study class was led by one of the church elders, Bill Harder. Attendance would vary, depending on who was in church on that particular day, but there was a core group of about seven that regularly attended. The topics could be about a particular Bible chapter or verse or a book that Bill might have brought in to read and discuss. As I studied, learned, discussed, and understood more about the multitude of topics, history, and the subject at hand, namely Christianity, the more I started to feel my place. I approached it with an intellectual curiosity that I've always possessed, and in so doing possibly became a voice, even if it were a new one. I started to feel more at home, but I wasn't there yet.

Back to late 2005 when I was looking for work again... A staffing agency found my resume "on the internet" and requested an interview with me regarding a position as an advisor for an online university. I was intrigued but a little skeptical. After the interview with the staffing agency, I interviewed with one of the directors of admissions at American Intercontinental University. The position was a hybrid of salesman and counselor. I would have to recruit students who were looking for a way to earn a degree without having to attend a physical campus. I was never really a salesman and was somewhat inconsistent with that part of the role. I was better at preparing students for class, academically, financially, and sometimes psychologically. Being a "for profit" entity, it was always difficult for me to balance the university's demand for more students to meet profit margins and the demand to prepare them so that they have a better chance for graduation, which helps to keep the University in good graces with their accreditor, which makes them legitimate in the eyes of the Department of Education. I was accustomed to the not-for-profit pace of the Chicago City College system where the students came to us and we served them accordingly. It would be an understatement to say that at AIU, we proactively sought out students who contacted us directly or indirectly through various third-party marketing sites. After a few months, I had to go out on an unqualified leave of absence due to a pressure sore. Unqualified - meaning no benefits and no income. Technically, since I was not past their 90-day temporary or probationary period, I was still a temporary employee, but they hired me back in June 2006 after I had healed. I learned and progressed through the advisor ranks. They gave the positions different titles through the years but promotions were based on the achievement of quantity and quality. Doing well in this position was and still is a springboard to management, but I never aspired to that. I moved to the reentry admissions department in 2013, which assisted students who had previously attended and were no longer enrolled for a multitude of reasons. It was my job to help them get back and become successful again. The best part of this move was that I no longer had to play the role of salesman.

I've always had trouble describing, in "able-bodied" terms, how the various symptoms and effects of this condition actually make me feel. Through the years, I've been hospitalized many times to try to figure out what was causing whatever a certain problem du jour was. It was during one such hospital stay in 2007 that I developed my first major pressure sore that would require reconstructive surgery. I don't remember the actual reason I was even admitted, but apparently, from lack of turning in the bed, I developed a sore on my side and was told by the nurse upon discharge from the hospital to have it checked out by my doctor. Well, it only looked like a little scab, so I didn't do anything about it for several weeks. I thought it should have healed by then, so I finally went to see my doctor. I don't think ironic is the right word, but I think it's funny that as much as I was, and still am to this day, reluctant to go to the doctor, I sure have spent and spend a lot of time there! The doctor lifted up the scab and discovered a deep tunnel that almost reached my hip bone. He said I would need a specialist to treat this and would probably require surgery. My long-time doctor from the RIC, Dr. Elliot Roth, referred me to Dr. Victor Lewis from Northwestern Memorial Hospital, a renowned plastic surgeon. I wondered what a plastic surgeon had to do with fixing a hole in my side when I didn't need a face lift or implants of any kind until it was explained to me that plastic surgeons also reconstruct wounds of various types. Dr. Lewis was one of the innovators of the technique called "flap surgery." The surgeon would go into the wound, cut out the necrotic (dead) tissue, delicately move live tissue from a nearby donor area, and then close the whole thing with a flap of some sort. They opened up my side from my hip to my knee in order to get enough donor tissue to fill the deep hole in my side. Unfortunately, this wouldn't be my last experience with this innovative type of surgery. The next time or two it would get me in the end though, literally. No, not the end as in "the end." The end as in where I sit. Not a good thing for a person who uses a wheelchair all the time.

The actual surgery has never been the hardest part about having surgery. It's the recovery. After the surgery, I had to lie flat on my back in a special bed for two weeks. Sitting up would split everything open. The bed was basically a specialized air mattress that circulated silicon particles, keeping the patient virtually weightless and floating in the bed. The almost 100% reduction of pressure and constant airflow facilitated the healing. At this point in my history, it's almost comical to say that the repercussions of that particular situation weren't as serious as they could have been. The recovery time for this reconstruction was nothing at all compared to what it could have been. Had the deep pressure sore been where I sit, it would have been a lot more serious. I would learn just how serious in just a few short years. One would think that after all this, I would have a good case against the hospital for negligence in that they weren't turning me properly to avoid pressure sores. My general physician, Dr. Fred Halloran, even referred me to his lawyer. Unfortunately, I blew it again. The lawyer advised that because I had let five weeks pass before I saw Dr. Halloran, and eventually Dr. Roth and Dr. Lewis, I was culpable for "comparative negligence." He also advised Dr. Halloran not to put his name on any legal papers because of the possibility of losing visitation rights at that hospital. I was disappointed but understood the logic.

I had a couple of other bad breaks in those days, bones these times. On separate occasions, I broke my left ankle and left femur. My caregiver at that time dropped me while transferring me to my wheelchair, and my leg caught underneath me, snapping my left femur. I broke the tibia and fibula in several places in my ankle when I let the lift of my van down on an uneven surface, causing me to tumble out of my wheelchair, dragging and twisting my ankle behind me.

Along with my past injuries, both ankles and both femurs have been broken. How many people can say that?

Despite my physical maladies, life seemed to be improving. I was working and earning a decent salary, although not what I would call a comfortable one, and I found the place where I could worship and learn and grow my Christianity. I was meeting more people and developing new friendships, but I was beginning to think that I should be doing more. I noticed people making a lot of effort to make the services run smoothly who were not employed by the church. This told me I should also be doing something, but I had no idea what because everybody I saw was doing something that required more physical ability than I possess. The ushers passed out papers, passed around the collection plate, walked up and down the aisles for various reasons... All things I physically had trouble with. The elders who were on duty would assist with communion and would be there for anything else that needed to be done, as well as the behind-the-scenes things they did that I would eventually learn about. I bemoaned my problem to my new friend Wendy because I was feeling guilty about being just a "taker" and not a "giver" of any kind, financial contributions notwithstanding. Not knowing my background, she retorted, "You can write, can't you? Write something about yourself that we can send to our college kids and military members who can be warned and inspired by your story." I may have paraphrased that quote, but that was the essence of it. I wrote up a little piece that was included in the packages the Keeping in Touch (K.I.T.) ministry would send out. I realize that wasn't all that much of a contribution, but it was a start.

By this time, the pump that had been implanted into my abdomen a few years back was really doing its job of controlling the muscle spasms. That was great, but it also ruined the rest of my body. The muscle tone in my abdomen and lower back went to zilch. Not only did this affect my trunk balance, the lack of muscle tone started allowing for the movement and shifting of my intestines, or my guts, one could say. My mother might refer to them as one's "innards." This shift literally started pulling me to my left and caused pretty significant scoliosis. The fabulous tone in my legs and butt that allowed me to wear shorts sometimes went bye-bye also, leaving my legs to look like pencils. The tone in my butt had provided a cushion between skin and bone that would no longer be there and prove to be very problematic. Not fun, but the side effects were a necessary evil if I were to function. While never a day has gone by without pain, I mentioned that there are worse things the body can do to itself than pain. Cold sweat ranks at the top of my worst list. Sweat is one of those autonomic functions under the auspices of the sympathetic nervous system that we don't control by thinking. As we all know, its purpose is to cool our bodies when we generate internal or feel external heat. There are many internal and external triggers in my body that can cause me to sweat when I'm not hot in any way. Adding to the problem is the difficulty in diagnosing why the cold sweat occurs, other than something blatantly obvious such as a pressure sore. Not only do I get a cooling effect when I don't need it, usually there is an indescribable feeling inside that I can only attempt to define as an electrical charge going in and out of my body.

I start to shake and shiver and if there is a good song on in the background, I might start to dance to the beat.

I finally decided to become a member of Immanuel Lutheran in 2008 after three years of riding the fence. I took the new member class that gave me the basics on what it was to be a member, along with some church history...nothing really intense. The class was taught by Fred Siebert, a volunteer and longtime member of Immanuel who would become a dear friend. It was also a time when the senior pastor of the church, Pastor Ed Doerner, answered a call to be the senior pastor at a church in Michigan. On top of that, I got a pressure sore that didn't require surgery, but required me to lie on my belly for a couple of weeks. One of the requirements for becoming a new member was to be presented in front of the congregation. I had completed the classes, but now when my classmates were presented, I was at home. I had really made up my mind to join this church and was quite disappointed about this technicality when the interim pastor, Pastor Tom Acton, came to visit. He told me he had spoken with the Board of Elders, and they agreed to bypass the technicality and welcomed me as a full-fledged member. He also announced that he answered the call to become the senior pastor at Immanuel. Holy cow! I had missed a lot in my absence!

2010 is the year I had the first reconstructive flap surgery where I sit, right in the sweet spot outside of the anus where the top of the thigh meets the butt. This sore tunneled down almost to the bone and would need some donor flesh from my now atrophied bottom, once known as the gluteus maximus... maybe mine should now be called the gluteus minimus! After the surgery, I had to lie on my back for two weeks in that same type of special bed I described earlier when I had this type of surgery on my hip. I don't like to admit it, but those first two weeks were virtual torture. Lying on my back 24/7 except to turn ever so slightly in the morning to "do my business" was so humiliating and mentally challenging that I could only put on the mask of false bravado and make sick jokes about myself as a means of dealing with it. But then I had to be moved to the RIC for another two weeks to get the newly reconstructed area in good enough condition to withstand sustained sitting again. It would take several months of slowly increasing my sitting time before I could return to work, even part-time. At least at the RIC I could get out of my bed and go to therapies and do a lot of exercising. I tried to make the most of my time spent there and actually enjoyed the opportunity to use their equipment. I had and still have a hand crank exercise machine at home, but the stuff at the RIC was much more technologically advanced and up-to-date.

After a few months of following the process, I returned to work. AIU had always valued me and would welcome me back from short-term disability leave on more than one occasion while I was under their employment. There were times when I exceeded the federally protected Family Medical Leave Act (FMLA) timeframe and they could have released me. It probably wouldn't have looked good, but I don't want to entertain any other cynical thought. By now, I had learned how to become enough of a salesman along with being a good advisor to be able to keep my job so far. It was a very demanding position and there was a high turnover. Advisors came and went and that meant new friends did the same. I really try to be good-natured and exude positivity whenever possible, but my personality never really meshed with the "rah-rah" atmosphere of a sales environment, which the enrolling students aspect of the job was. High achievers were always rewarded. There were times when I did very well and times when I couldn't enroll a student to save my life. I kept at it but was very frustrated throughout the years. We were also measured and evaluated by the number of students who started and continued into their programs. There were many factors beyond our control, but nevertheless, they were part of the equation and we were required to meet or exceed expectations. Each team of about 15 to 20 advisors was led by a director of admissions, or DOA, whose job it was to get the most out of his or her advisors in order to meet the requirements of the University. It was a pressure-filled environment for all, but each director had his or her own style and way of doing things within the University guidelines. Of course, sometimes a rogue DOA might try to maneuver outside of those guidelines but eventually would be discovered and probably dismissed. My successes came when the particular director of my team recognized my strengths and weaknesses, encouraged me, and had my back. I didn't do well under a micromanager or loudmouth "boiler room" type manager.

After a few years, I had overcome many of my weaknesses and achieved enough to rank among the top advisors. I was able to get on the top performing team that was led by a director who was the opposite of a micromanager and got the most out of his advisors because we always knew he had our backs if we did what we were supposed to do. He didn't get on you if you failed, as long as you were putting in the required effort. He did try to help you if you needed it. If you were on Brian Sathern's team in those days, you must have been doing okay. Everything was going along just swimmingly for a while. I was on the best team. I had the best schedule. I had the best boss. I was easily making the numbers with enrollments and starts, so I didn't have the stress of imminently losing my job. Circumstances would soon change. The longtime director of the reentry admissions department was fired because she was overheard disparaging a vice president on an open phone line. Brian was asked to take over the reentry team, leaving his second-in-command, Matt, in charge of the team. The position he had held under Brian had different titles over the years, usually something like student manager. Everybody thought Matt would have the same management style as Brian because he had been under his mentorship for a couple of years. Nothing could be further from the truth. Matt was the ultimate micromanager. This management style and other discouraging incidents negatively impacted my performance, and ultimately my frame of mind. It got to where I almost reached my breaking point. When I knew I couldn't take it anymore, a couple of opportunities opened up on Brian's reentry team. I went through the whole interview process and was subsequently hired for one of the positions. Although the demand was much higher on the reentry team, the available population of previous students we were targeting made it possible to meet that demand. Also, working under Brian's management style again made it a lot easier to do my job. This was 2013 and it would turn out to be one of those "good year-bad year" situations again for me.

Chapter 8: Getting Beyond Health Issues

Soon after Brian hired me for the reentry team, I had to give in to a persistent pressure sore that had worked itself down to the bone again in the same place as 2010. I was running out of flesh on that side of my butt to donate to myself, but the surgery had to be done. I had also developed a pressure sore on the other side that had a much larger surface area but wasn't as deep. The plan was to do each one in separate surgeries because of the healing process. Trying to heal two reconstructed sites at the same time would be too taxing on the body and therefore, counterproductive. When I informed Brian that I would be out for a few months, he said, "You could have told me before I hired you," and then he gave me a sly grin and said he would have hired me anyway.

Dr. Lewis, along with his team of resident surgeons, performed the surgery again at Northwestern Memorial Hospital in Chicago. This was the best place to be as a quadriplegic patient, along with its affiliated rehabilitation hospital, the Rehabilitation Institute of Chicago, now known as the Shirley Ryan AbilityLab. If you had to be hospitalized, even if you're not a quadriplegic patient, this was, and is, the place to be. The surgery went well, but a few days later I started feeling the symptoms of a urinary tract infection. A urine sample was sent to the lab and it came back positive. They prescribed an antibiotic that was supposed to clear it up in a few days but had no effect. I remember feeling dumbfounded about having a UTI at this time when I remembered that I had been feeling very mild symptoms of what I thought could have been a UTI before I had surgery. The problem with this is that those symptoms can be many things, so I usually would put off going to the doctor until the symptoms became more severe and there was no doubt in my mind. With all the hullabaloo of surgery and recovery, I had completely forgotten about the mild symptoms. Right after surgery, the standard procedure is to put the patient on IV prophylactic antibiotics to prevent infection at the wound site during the first few days after surgery. I was taken off of whatever antibiotic it was after a few days, and that's when I think my previous infection came raging back, now more resistant to antibiotics. In no way do I blame the hospital for my ensuing nightmare. All fault lies squarely on the shoulders of one person, the chief resident doctor, whose name I don't remember and don't care to remember. I can't recall the specific time period, but over the next several days or so, the infection raged on and none of the antibiotics they tried had any effect.

By this time, my symptoms were so severe that I was visibly shaking and cold sweating profusely. Also, my bladder was continually spasming and only putting out a few drops at a time. I instructed the nurse to insert an indwelling catheter to do the work of the bladder and reduce my symptoms. I knew from previous experience what would help, and the nurse thought it was logical but said she had to get a doctor's order. Dr. Lewis wasn't available so she needed to get the order from the chief resident. He was a very "by the book" practitioner and denied the request because indwelling catheters in clinical environments can lead to urinary tract infections. Hey doc, I already had one of those! Listen to your patient! He still refused and my suffering continued.

My family and friends continued to visit, of course, and they were shocked at my condition. I tried to get one of the other residents to write the order, but they all seemed to be intimidated by the chief resident and wouldn't go over his head, even if they agreed with me. Finally, one evening one of the residents probably couldn't stand to witness my suffering any longer and wrote the order to insert a catheter. Immediately, the bladder spasms stopped and I felt some sense of relief. At the same time, they found an antibiotic that could only be prescribed by their disease control specialist doctors and only used it in rare circumstances. The threat of resistant bacteria from overusing and misusing antibiotics was a danger the doctors were trying to prevent. They finally "broke the glass" on this last-ditch effort antibiotic and soon thereafter, my UTI went away and they removed the catheter. What a huge difference! No more shivering! I would still get cold sweats from other stimuli at times, but they were less severe now. I wasn't the only one who was furious with the chief resident for needlessly putting me through that suffering by not listening to me. I'm not going to request having a catheter inserted into me unless it were absolutely necessary! Kelly was furious and wanted the young doctor's medical license. He wanted to report him to higher authorities, as Dr. Lewis was already aware. Dr. Lewis said he had a long conversation with the young doctor and impressed upon him the need to practice the "art of medicine" as well as the science of medicine. He told him that included listening to a patient who has as much knowledge and experience as me. He asked us to allow him to learn from this and not try to ruin his career. I agreed that this would be the Christian thing to do. My brother also agreed to back off but was still seething for a while. Now that this was behind me, I would finally be able to heal and recover as normal. I was wrong of course.

With all of this going on, they decided not

to surgically repair the sore that was on the other side. It had never tunneled down very deep but had covered a large surface area that was now healing. Unfortunately, with all the present circumstances and the way I had to lie on my back in this special bed 24/7, except for the slight turn I was allowed to go to the bathroom, the surgical site became infected. Dr. Lewis and his team had to open it up to clear out the infection and re-staple it closed. This set me back approximately two weeks. The physical demand it took to lie like that in one position for so long was clearly something that can be overwhelming, but for me, the mental demand was far more challenging. If I didn't have visitors and wasn't being attended to by hospital staff, the only mental stimuli I had was the television. I have nothing against television, but I preferred to read whenever I was hospitalized in the past. In this case, that was impossible. After a total of a month of lying on my back, I was ready to be moved down the block on Superior Street in downtown Chicago to the Rehabilitation Institute of Chicago, the number one rehabilitation hospital in the nation year after year. Before they moved me over there, a couple of their physical therapists came over and sat me up on the side of my now standard hospital bed to see if I could tolerate sitting for a brief time. I immediately broke a profuse cold sweat, but this was to be expected with such extensive surgery on one side of my bottom and the still healing pressure sore on the other. I think the circulating air of the special bed I spent so much time in accelerated that healing process and now I was ready to continue recovering and get to work at the RIC.

After a couple of weeks of rehabilitation at the RIC, which basically consisted of getting accustomed to functioning on a daily basis again, I went home but wouldn't be able to sit long enough to return to work for several more months. I had worked myself back into good cardiovascular condition and strengthened and toned my "un-paralyzed" muscles by utilizing the RIC's exercise machines and wrap-around free weights. There were other patients around me who would become dismayed by the amount of work and pain required to rehabilitate effectively, and some who were just plain lazy, but I knew that giving up would only invite more problems to this already crowded party. Dr. Roth told me that I had made good use of my time there. That's high praise coming from him! He put me on strict sitting limitations, gradually increasing as the weeks and months went by. I tried to stay true to his instructions, but my impatience may have caused me to accelerate my sitting times by just a little bit. Regardless, he was not going to sign off on an eight-hour day until he was comfortable enough with my healing. I could easily reopen everything if I jumped the gun too soon. Throughout my history, it has been a balance between the mental and physical. The physical limitations of my condition have continually sapped my mental strength. The knowledge of not being able to do the simplest of things has always been the devil on my shoulder, if you will. Making wise decisions that don't necessarily benefit my desire has been the angel on the other shoulder. Not that desire is always a bad thing; it can just take over at times.

The people from my church were very supportive. I remember having several of them visit me in the hospital, including a couple of elders. The future senior pastor, when he was Associate Pastor Warren Schilf, was also a visitor and turning into a good friend. I knew by then that Immanuel was the place where I wanted to grow my faith. I was inspired by the open arms of the people I met to want to learn more and give back more. I started attending another Bible study on Saturday morning, which I still attend to this day. Herb Hetzel, who would become a good and dear friend, led this morning Bible study. We would read from the Bible or other resources that covered a vast area of study. There was so much to learn! The history, the extra-biblical perspective of our faith, that archaeology, and many other topics were covered. A few of the guys liked the way I read and strongly suggested that I volunteer to be a Scripture reader during services. I appreciated the compliment, but this was way outside of my comfort zone. I had no intention or desire to get in front of a few hundred people and read actual Bible verses. The wording can be very tricky. Some of the names of the people and places are virtually impossible to pronounce. I had made speeches and presentations to various audiences throughout my life, but this was different. I didn't want to mess up. I didn't have much choice, though. John Love, one of the Bible study participants, recommended and referred me to the church office. There was no turning back from there. I was asked if I would agree to be put in the rotation. It wasn't all that bad as I only had to read every six weeks or so, but I made sure I was prepared when it was my turn by looking up the difficult pronunciations of people and places. I think it would surprise many people to learn that I don't like being in front of people or being on stage. Reading Scripture in front of the congregation puts one on stage, in person and broadcast online. I think it's important to get it right to convey the intended message. Although always forgivable, if the reader flubs it up, it doesn't benefit the congregation much. I don't get nervous up there. I'm just uncomfortable in my own skin. I certainly don't do it because I want to. I do it because I'm called to. I don't do as much as I used to, but I'm called to do other things so I don't feel guilty!

I know Dr. Roth wanted me to take a little longer, but he consented to sign the paperwork to release me to return to work part-time for the first two weeks. Part-time equals part pay so I wanted to get back to work full-time as soon as possible, but I also wanted to be sure I was sufficiently healed enough to tolerate a full day of sitting. Everything held up, so I returned to work full-time and hit the ground running, pardon the expression. I guess I'm actually better at helping students solve their problems than trying to sell them on a concept. For several years moving forward, things at work went exceptionally well. There was a pretty tight bond on the team because there wasn't much turnover like there was in general admissions. At that time, most of the advisors were the best of the University and had the most experience. Like anything else in life, there would be change. Brian would be asked to manage other teams that might be floundering because he seemed to have a way of motivating people without browbeating them. I served under the pleasure of several more directors during my time there, a few were actually great, but we never had the same mojo after Brian left for browner pastures!

All the while, I was feeling more confident

of my place along my faith journey. One of my Saturday morning Bible study co-participants, Dan Klaman, asked me if I would fill a spot on his usher team because one of the volunteers had to quit for some reason. Now, wait just a second here! Reading Scripture and being uncomfortable in front of people is one thing, but this was completely different. Handing out bulletins, passing the collection tray, and guiding people in and out of the sanctuary are some of the responsibilities of ushers. The thought of trying to hand anything to anybody with my paws and the thought of fumbling and dropping whatever it may be made my chest and throat clutch with anxiety. Dan assured me that we would figure it out. I'm not going to say I finally got it right or even knew what I was doing, but I think I was getting better at being a Christian. I was moving along on my journey, but I still had a long way to go.

I know it's not a coincidence that for the next decade, while not perfect or even wonderful, things in my life were much better. By no means do I think I was being rewarded for good behavior, but the focus on wanting and trying to be good kept the focus away from wanting to be bad, which didn't take much trying at all. The more I gave of myself, the more I got back in return. Exactly what the Bible says... you reap what you sow. I'm not talking about financial help necessarily, there were avenues to resources for that if necessary, but the love I would feel and still feel from a like-minded group of people was very comforting indeed. I think by this point in my life, it was more important to me to be a part of something greater than myself than to keep following the selfish path I was previously taking.

After a few years of being a member and feeling like I actually found my place, Tim Laabs of the nominating committee asked if I would be interested in running for the elder board. Elder was, and still is, an elected position and would have to be voted on by the congregation. I thought he must be kidding. Here I am, the new kid on the block, being asked to run for a leadership position in the church. Me? A leader in a church? Who am I kidding? I knew in my heart that my faith had grown through the years and I had learned much about a lot. Regardless, elders were required to do physical and grunt work around the church and I'm not capable of much of that. Tim assured me that there would be other things I would be asked to do that wouldn't require physical ability. The main goal of an elder is to support the spiritual health of the congregation. That can be interpreted in many ways, but being a positive force and being available for congregation members to speak with about whatever they need to speak about is what's important. With all of the responsibilities elders are required to fulfill, it's not easy to persuade eligible members to run. It's very rare that there are more nominees than positions, so I was duly elected along with all the other candidates!

I am so thankful for Immanuel Lutheran Church here in Palatine. I have friends and family all over the place but no one in near proximity, so it's wonderful to have a place only a mile from my home where I can go to worship, serve, and fellowship with a new set of friends I never thought I would be so glad to see! I was still working with reentry admissions in those years after 2013, but I didn't find my job to be fulfilling. Yes, I am aware that I helped some people along the way, but even in reentry, the grind and lack of reward for what is put into the job can have an effect on anyone. It wasn't AIU and what their goals were; it was the students. There were some who bought into the process and program and appreciated what we did as advisors, but many of them were not always necessarily nice to work with. I could handle it, but after years of truly giving my best, I yearned for something else in life. By this time, I hadn't written anything professionally for at least 20 years and I was feeling guilty about it, actually. I wasn't too naïve or blind to see that the communications world had passed me by. I don't remember the exact year, but one Sunday, after hearing a particularly eloquent sermon by Pastor Tom, I commented to him that I needed to get back into writing and get creative again. The only response I got was something nonverbal like "mm-hmm." Thanks a lot of Pastor Tom.

On the following Sunday after the service, I was approached by Diana Broj, Immanuel's former program or project director. I think the name of her position was program director, but as our budget hasn't allowed for that for many years, I could be wrong.

Anyway, she asked me if I would be interested in writing for the church newsletter after hearing from Pastor Tom that I have a background in writing and was interested in doing something. Sly Pastor Tom, sIy. I was actually amused because I had been thinking of more selfish projects such as articles I might get paid for, but this actually appealed to me as I would be able to use whatever talent I still had for the benefit of the church... something greater than myself. I told Diana I hadn't written anything in 20 years and was sure I was rusty but was willing to give it a try. She said we would take it slowly and easily at first and go from there. If I recall correctly, the first article was mostly about me and my faith journey, so it wasn't too hard, but my fears were unnecessary as it all came back to me quite easily. Each month, I would get a topic and possibly a resource person to talk to about it. After that, it was up to me to put together something interesting and of course, something in line with the church's overall message. Talk about trust!

The more I became involved and immersed myself in matters of the church, the more distracted I became from my own disability, although it would never go away of course. The physical aspects were impossible to ignore. It was the mental ones I could control a little bit with positivity. When I get among other people, I try to be a beacon of that positivity and perhaps, hope. Sometimes I do have to put on a false mask, but it stopped being one of bravado. Even if something would bring me down, no matter what the cause, I tried not to present negativity to others.

Chapter 9: Life Goes On

Work was going very well. Our team was a tightly knit group as there was not a lot of turnover and was comprised of mostly well-seasoned veterans. I was so grateful that Brian hired me because I was getting burned out in general admissions. I have to admit, my team spoiled me, especially the women. They looked out for me way above and beyond any kind of duty. As the years went on and very little change in personnel occurred, my colleagues became more like friends, at least several of them did. Brian would sometimes arrange for off-site teambuilding exercises when the university would allow it. Other directors had done this and still do, but I felt a sense of unity and friendship on this team. This seemed to lead to a more genuinely good time had by all who participated in these routine-breaking activities.

As much as I actually enjoyed my job

through those years, it wasn't something that I would call career fulfilling. When I was hired, I thought it might be an upward career move and not just a job because of the educational aspect of the position. I certainly didn't understand this new industry and I had no idea I was getting myself into such a competitive environment. I *was* just doing a job. There's no shame to it. I was doing what I had to do, but I wouldn't say I was extremely happy doing it. Don't get me wrong. Working for AIU was a dream compared to working for the bank. I just never found a way to become the professional writer I had always aspired to be. I was thankful for the opportunity to lend my talents to the church by writing articles for the newsletter, but that didn't fulfill my career aspirations either. I think that the more I became involved with my church, the less the need or desire I had for career fulfillment. By this time, I had reached my 50s and was no longer very driven to ascend any type of corporate ladder. There were a few opportunities available at AIU outside of management, but I never seemed to be in the right place at the right time for those, or I was just unaware. Management was the most direct route if I wanted to try to move up in the ranks. I never had any desire to be someone's boss, even in my younger days, so that was not the path for me.

After 2013, there weren't any major health issues or catastrophes that required me to bounce back up from being knocked down. The biggest challenge for me was to just keep moving forward as my condition seemed to get progressively worse, or at least the symptoms of it were. Many of the very unpleasant and even painful feelings I had experienced throughout the years seemed to be more exaggerated as the years flew by. I would continue to have minor skin issues where I sit, such as scratches and tears that, even if very small, would require me to stay off of my butt for a few days or weeks, depending on the severity. This is when my mind would go to the darkest places. I may not have been thrilled about how my career had turned out, but when these issues prevented me from working, I would tend to panic and feel anxious.

I lost my mom in 2016. At 91, she succumbed to pneumonia. She had battled it the year before, especially so she could attend the wedding of one of her granddaughters, but this time it was too much for her. She had lived a full and productive life, and we, as her children, were blessed to have her as our mother. My family all banded together in her final hours and my friends, both lifelong and newfound, joined us in celebrating her life. I know she had faith, so I know she has joined our Lord in paradise, along with my dad who was supposed to be waiting in heaven with a vodka gimlet and the next dance.

Throughout my life after my accident, I was simply amazed that I was attractive to women at all and that I was able to have girlfriends and even get married. But even after my divorce and the bad relationship that followed, I still had hope that I might meet someone whom I could fall in love with and would fall in love with me. Every time I even tried to ask someone out on a date though, her eyes would get has wide as a deer's caught in the headlights of an oncoming vehicle as she stammered out some kind of excuse or another.

I had been attracted to a woman at my church, whose name I won't use because I know she wouldn't want me to, for several years but never had the courage to ask her out. We had gone out to lunch as friends a few times, but I finally asked her if she wanted to go out on a real date and she said, "why not?" We dated a couple of times and things seemed to be going great. I was on top of the world because I thought we had embarked on a new relationship that would only grow when she abruptly called it off. I was devastated! I thought I had been blessed with a chance at love again at last, but I was sorely mistaken. She wouldn't give a real reason, only the old "it's not you; it's me" excuse. I felt such an intense feeling of loss and despair from this rejection, almost as bad as when my ex-wife announced her intention to divorce me. The love I had for my ex-wife was certainly deeper than this, but the possibility of having love again after thinking it was only remotely possible was what made it so powerful. I know I moped around for weeks afterward. It was difficult to focus on work, and despite my colleagues' best efforts, no one could raise my spirits. I had to go if I wanted to keep my job, but I had no desire to go anywhere else or do anything I enjoyed doing. I recognized the signs of depression and I knew I couldn't allow myself to fall into that abyss but I knew I couldn't do it alone. Church was my salvation. I always went to church. I never needed to make an excuse not to attend because I always wanted to attend. I could also go to the morning Bible study on Saturday morning, along with other events and services. It was hard to feel sorry for myself when I was around my family and friends. I know Dave had to "talk me off the ledge" on those evenings when I would call him up feeling so forlorn. My family and friends were, and still are, God's messengers, even if they didn't realize it.

I eventually got over that woman, but I never forgot her. Time marched on. I continued working, and though the thrill of a satisfying career experience was not there, I gave my best to my students and my employer. Whenever I felt like slacking off, I would think of how I would feel if I were paying me. I knew the programs and the process backward and forward and was able to adapt to the constant changes and updates to both throughout the years, so I know I was able to give good guidance to my students while representing the university in a professional and uplifting manner. The daily back and forth grind of going to an office workspace may have been inconvenient and sometimes difficult at times, but I know that the relationships and interaction I had with my colleagues were part of what kept me going. The end of the decade was fast approaching, and little did we know what the new menace was on the horizon.

Covid hit us in 2020. I don't even need to explain what that is, as the virus became part of everyone's everyday lives. We were sent to work from home in March of that year with the expectation that things would get back to normal in a few weeks or months and that we would return soon. We never did. It was definitely more convenient to work from home, but the isolation and loneliness from not interacting with our colleagues had a very depressing effect on many of us, including myself. A whole lot of new guidelines and rules were instituted throughout the land to try to control the disease. The physical campus of the church and school were shut down requiring students and congregation members to attend classes and services exclusively online. I was an elder at the time and we did our best to provide uplifting and also entertaining services while our school staff worked diligently to provide instruction to our students online so they wouldn't fall so far behind. It was a difficult time for everybody but after a vaccine was developed and distributed, things slowly got back to a "new normal."

As the years went by came the stark realization that I had far outlived what I had always thought would be my life expectancy. This was new territory for my psyche. I had always thought that I would check out somewhere in my 40s from something just taking over my compromised system. People with severe spinal cord injuries are now living longer due to a number of factors, especially advances in medicine and rehabilitation. The Shirley Ryan AbilityLab is a huge modern facility two blocks south on Erie Street from where the RIC was. It is the epitome of research, rehabilitation, and teaching in rehabilitative medicine. I still see Dr. Roth at least once a year and participate in as many studies or surveys that may be appropriate for my situation. Generally, I'm in good health, although I feel the advancement of years with gravity weighing down on my spine, causing the arthritis in my neck to torment me in my old age! I have arthritis in other areas where I broke bones, but those aches and pains don't bother me as much.

Still, I would keep going forward as much as I could. As the decade quickly advanced, I kept working and participating in my church. I would soon exceed the term limit as an elder and was looking forward to some relaxation from any kind of board duty. I knew I would still be writing articles for the newsletter and doing other things for the church as needed. Not so fast! Tim Laabs from the nominating committee called me up one day to see if I would be interested in running for the school board, officially known as the Board of the Christian School (BCS). I told him I didn't know if I would be a good fit because I didn't have kids and didn't know much about the school. He said that is exactly why I was being asked. The nominating committee thought I would have no agenda and no preconceived notions. While serving on the school board turned out to be more of a challenge than I ever thought it would, I'm just glad I was even thought of and had the opportunity to serve in some way.

In January 2023, we lost my good friend, Nick Pasquini. He had been fighting a form of blood cancer for several years. None of our group of friends thought it would work out that way. After my accident, everybody always thought I would be the first to go. Not only did I always seem to get myself into deadly situations, the mortality statistics relating to my condition dictated such thought. Nick lost his battle because, I think, he just gave up. He was a gifted drummer and one of the guys I had known since we were freshmen in high school. He always won awards for his playing along with Dave on the saxophone. I have many fond memories of Nick and will continue to miss him.

Chapter 10: Conclusion

As the years have gone by, that mustard seed of faith that was once planted deep inside of me has now grown quite a bit. I'm not going to say that makes me a good man or a good Christian or a good anything, but I am trying to get better at all of those things, although I'm not really sure what it means to be a "good anything." To be honest, the only thing in my life I always thought I could take credit for was my strength, or resiliency. I've never allowed myself to give up and always wondered where that drive came from. I liked to take credit for being the big, tough Irishman, but I finally understood how weak "he" really was. I was finally able to take off the mask of false bravado. I always heard this unspoken voice within that told me to get up, no matter what. I never knew why it was there, but I did like to take credit for it. I realize why I always believed and always said why there was no choice. It wasn't my voice I was listening to; it was the Lord's. I had always wanted to hear that deep, booming voice I would immediately know as God's that would tell me what to do and that everything would be all right, but that's not the way it works. It took me a long time to realize that it couldn't possibly be my voice because the result was the one thing I never seemed to screw up, my recovery or bouncing back. I always came back for more! Remember how the Frisbee used to bean me in the face and I kept on playing?

I'm going to contradict myself and say I've always had a choice. If I chose to ignore the voice and gave in to the temptation of quitting, it might have been easier than the hard work required in the short run, but in the long run, I'm sure I would not have made it as far. I know that if I don't continue to listen to the voice and keep trying, bad things will happen. Giving up means breaking down. Everything breaks down... body, mind, spirit. I can't say I never give up or quit anything. Never is an absolute and nobody is perfect. The only human who was ever perfect was Jesus of course, but being God incarnate, one would expect that! I'll always regret quitting the freshman high school football team. Sure, throughout my life there have been many trivial abandonments of whatever I was pursuing, but that sticks out in my mind. It confirms my belief that it is better to see something through to the end, whatever it may be. Then there are no regrets. Easier said than done. It's not always easy to finish the job. Most of the time, it's hard enough to even start it. I believe we all have the ability to put forth the effort it takes to get up after being knocked down. I believe that God installed a multitude of programs in us through our DNA, our genetic code. There is little difference among us all regarding these programs. I'm not telling people that their efforts are not enough or that they should be like me. I think it's up to each individual to determine if and when to activate their programs. I'm not talking about looks or artistic or athletic ability or intelligence; I'm talking about matters of the will. The hardest part of what happened to me and how I am is knowing that this is how it's going to be, no matter what. We have not yet figured out how to fix me, so I know things are not going to get better, only worse. It makes my skin crawl that I require another human being just to lift me out of bed in the morning to get the process started to be ready to face a new day. Of course, the physical aspect is very difficult, but it's the mental burden that weighs me down. I don't want to go through all this again and again. This is when I have to listen to that voice. Either I listen and I try to get up and function, or I ignore it and sink back into further misery.

The one thing I know in my heart I can take credit for without feeling vain is that I try. It's not difficult to find the motivation to put forth the effort for something I want to do. It is very different when it's something I know will be very unpleasant or even painful, but if I want to improve the circumstance, or even just survive, I know it's something I must do. This isn't anything noble or brave, although in my past I may have thought it was. I realized that the strength I always thought was my own was not mine at all, but the strength that God gave me. It was just up to me whether I wanted to use it. It goes back to when I was in traction with a broken neck. I knew I had to do something if I wanted to change my circumstance, through rehabilitation and education. I can look back on my life and say, "At least I tried."

I recently retired a few years early, not because of accomplishment or deservedness, but because in the past few years, I just started feeling my body wearing out in response to these new and/or exaggerated symptoms I've been experiencing. I felt it was necessary to conserve the energy I had left to pursue other interests and projects. After driving home from the office, and even after working from home following Covid, I would quickly eat something, brush my teeth, wash up, and immediately get out of my chair. Of course, the devil was dancing on my shoulder, crowing that I'm giving in and giving up, but the angel on my other shoulder reminded me that I'm conserving my strength and energy for other pursuits. Over the past almost 45 years since I've been injured, I've shared some of the tales I've written about here with many people and countless times have been told I should write a book about myself. Countless times I've refused because I knew I would have to delve into a number of unpleasant memories I would need to write about if I wanted to tell an honest story. I had an epiphany one day after sharing one such tale with Fred from church. After telling him I didn't want to write such a book, he said, "You know, you might just help somebody." That did it. It means that it wasn't all about me, even though the story pretty much was. I'm just an example. Everyone has the same program, but we were given the free will to activate it. That's where the choice is. Listen to your voice. It's probably not you talking.

1963 - Kevin, Diana, Laura, Kelly

1968 - Laura and Kevin. Trying to be Paul McCartney

1974 - Kevin at 14

1976 - Just saw Rocky - hitting the heavy bag in Dave's garage.

1976 - "Getting strong now...."

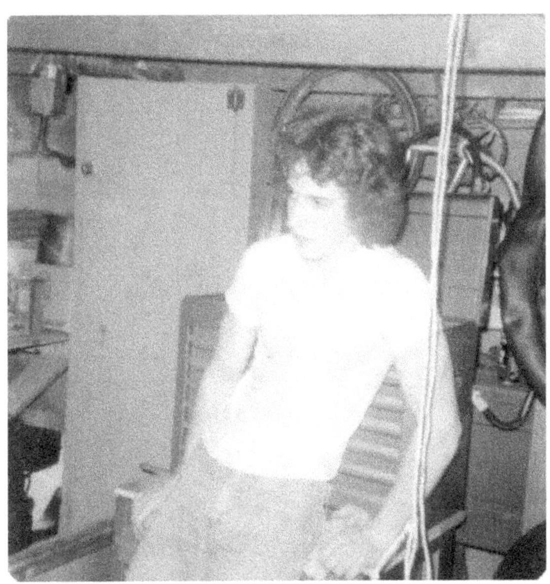

1976 - Taking a break

1978 - Greg, Dave, Kevin, Nick graduating high school

1978 - I was the only kid who could get up on the
Janesville, WI cow!

1979 - Kevin and Nick, 3 months before the accident.
Actors in Tom Scott's college film project

1979 - "We've been workin' on the railroad..." Can we
act, or what?

1980 - Trying to hold on to the tough guy image.

1984 or 1985 - My parents, Jim and Jinny

1984 - Laura, Kelly, Kevin, Diana at Laura's wedding.

1993 - Jonathan, Jeff, Nick, Dan at my wedding
celebration

1993 - Getting married but respecting Maggie's privacy.

2019 - Hanging out with Jeff, Kevin, Greg, Dave

2021 - Most of my family. Foster kids faces blurred out.